Trauma and Abuse Decoded: A Poor Person's Guide to a World-Class Healing.

Cover design by Dawnn Blalock and Blalock Imaging, LLC (www.allcustomphoto.com).
Technical support by Roger MacPherson.

ISBN: 978-0-615-58999-2

This book is dedicated in loving memory to Albert and Ruth.

My deepest gratitude to Steven, my editor and husband. Thank you for all of it.

My soulful thanks to Sr. Rossella Hein for inspiration, and Kate Holt for her love and friendship.

Special thanks to Dawnn Blalock for her advice, time, and expertise in designing the cover, and to Roger MacPherson for removing some of the mysteries of publishing that we encountered.

Blessed am I.

To have an experience is one thing.

To be educated about it another.

Here is the education you need to overcome the experience.

Recommendation

I was twenty-two years old when I first met Megan. I had taken a job at a residential treatment center as a crisis worker. I should have known better than to accept a job with the title "crisis" in it, but I had just graduated and I wanted experience in the field. Although I had previously worked as a women's advocate in a domestic violence shelter during college, I was utterly unprepared for the amount of vicarious trauma and compassion fatigue I would experience over the next two years. It was a difficult phase of my life. I knew with certainty that I was meant to pursue a career in social services, yet I couldn't seem to do the work without damage to my own spirit. I searched for a mentor to guide me. I found just that in Megan.

The first time I saw her she was dressed in a long, flowing dress of purple cotton. Her silver hair sparkled in the sunlight. Sporting tattoos and funky jewelry, she looked like a goddess with an edge. Despite our age difference, we quickly developed a deep friendship. I looked to her for advice and wisdom, and she provided both. As the trust between us grew, she told me the story of her trauma. As I moved on to different experiences in the field and graduate training, she shared with me the steps she had taken to heal herself.

Since that time, I have had the honor of helping numerous individuals find their own path of healing. In my work with traumatized individuals, Megan's wisdom continues to guide me. Now her vast knowledge and effective techniques are available to you. May her wisdom guide you to a sense of wholeness and renewed vitality.

Katherine Duncan Holt, PsyD

Table of Contents

Introduction

This is not a scholastic work. You will never find it published and probably never quoted in "The Journal of Personality and Social Psychology." Some technical terms are used where unavoidable, and other psychological terms are used in a more generic sense. Likewise, there will be what might be considered to be New-Agey language that was selected because it best and most simply illustrates commonly known but technically complex concepts. There are also therapeutic approaches that are not accepted, and are even disputed and rejected, by many mainstream disciplines.

All this said, this work is still the result of more than ten years research, experimentation, and application.

I wrote this book because of my own horrific history of trauma and abuse. At the time of my experiences there was little or no guidance available for the victims of these crimes. The mental health system, social services, and society's general attitude and ignorance in the 1970s about these situations could blame the victim more than the perpetrator. Solutions were ineffective, and remedies were nonexistent. To heal, I had to find my own way through a tangle of pain and rejection. I was not totally without support, but, still, I made most of that journey alone.

As I matured my ordeal caused me to think about all the people in prisons, shelters, and on the streets who had similar experiences, but lacked the ability or facilities to understand the causes and effects stemming from their backgrounds. I became increasingly concerned about them and their inability to break the dark spell of their abuse, and the resulting trauma.

The purpose of this book is to help those people of little or no means pull themselves up by making sense of their experience and response, and to offer the tools that helped me to live a normal and happy life, and to know peace.

If you have experienced trauma without abuse, the tools and information offered here will still help you.

My hope is that this book touches all who need it, and those who may not need it for themselves, but have family, friends, or clients in pain.

A warning, though. Some of the language herein is strong. Some of the situations described may seem extreme or absurd. Nonetheless, this book can help you.

My Story

My parents met in a psychiatric ward. This is not a silly plot contrivance in a soap opera. If it weren't true, I would be a different person. Hopefully, someone else would be writing this because, with or without me, it would still be needed.

Neither my mother nor my father was mentally or emotionally healthy, and I do not know if the passing decades have improved upon their individual conditions. Certainly they should never have married. Perhaps they should not have produced children.

Nevertheless, they did. And, in fact, they produced three of us.

Exposure to and experience in the mental health field leads me to argue that my mother is legitimately mentally ill. This is opinion, not a professional diagnosis. But I suspect that she may have suffered abuse of some kind, although what and to what extent I cannot say. There was certainly trauma involved. And a lot of drama. There has always been drama.

My father grew up in a horribly abusive and alcoholic family. Modern research shows that such conditions can be as generational as genes. Like his father before him, my father was brutal and had no boundaries when it came to abuse.

His son may be only a little better. My brother became a man who is nearly as brutal and abusive. He thinks this shows what a man he is.

I do not know how much of any of this has been passed on to his children.

My sister is a sometimes-recovering alcoholic who embraced some of our mother's victimhood and manipulative tactics as her own. She chooses sides based on what it will gain her. As there is little I can offer her, she can afford to hate me.

This is the traditional nuclear family I grew up with. Unstable as a bomb, and too close to fault lines for safety.

By the time my parents split up I had been molested, raped, beat, and mentally and emotionally abused. I was seriously traumatized. At fourteen I was a suicidal mess. I stayed that way for years.

But the moment my father left I was free to make every choice governing my life. Not every choice was good or right. Plenty were bad. I indulged in risky behavior, repeatedly putting myself in danger (unconsciously trying to recreate the situations I thought I was done with, but more on that later), and finding plenty of trouble.

But they were my own choices to make. That meant something to me.

I was twenty when my maternal grandfather suddenly died. Of all my family I was closest to him and loved him most. He had always been in my corner, but he died believing he had failed me. This became my greatest sorrow.

I decided to make his soul proud of me. I decided to do whatever it took to heal my life, even if I had to do it on my own. The mental health practices at that time were less than useless for me. Some even threatened to compound my problems, traumatizing me in new ways. This left me with few choices. To give up was never an option. I could not disappoint the spirit of my grandfather even further. Or I could explore the alternative and sometimes simplistic techniques offered in the profusion of self-help books published in that era, and attempt to practice the exercises they recommended. Any help was better than no help, and positive help is always better than the negative kind.

Surprisingly, with a little self-discipline and a lot of thought, by the time I reached my mid-twenties my life was not half bad. I had worked through some issues, had a good job, and was also reading tarot cards at street fairs. It was at one of these that I made a friend who happened to be a massage therapist.

I became her client, not knowing that it was the next step in my recovery.

Her massage transformed my life like nothing else had. Through bodywork I was able to release huge amounts of pain, fear, grief, terror, and anger from my energy. There were things for which I had no names that poisoned my body, mind, and spirit. I was able to let them go, too.

Massage healed so much in me and brought me the unity within myself that I had not had. Its impact was so profound that, several years later, I chose massage therapy as my career. It helped me recognize the oneness of the body, the mind, and the spirit. In both my practice and in this book, I treat the three as one.

I am a trained and licensed massage therapist, and an artist. I have been a waitress and tarot card reader. All of these brought me to study and know humans for all that we are and can be. Because of all of this, the suffering of those whose histories include trauma and abuse has my heart.

A few paragraphs back, I accused my sister of embracing her "victimhood." A harsher truth for me to face is that I was a victim, same as she. True, terrible, inhumane things were done to us. Those experiences created someone that I never wanted to be. I was a victim.

One of the things that put people off when it comes to victims is their sometimes willingness to remain victims. I believe this circumstance occurs when members of this group develop a sense of helplessness and hopelessness. They don't have the tools, guidance, or strength to change. They may have been legitimately failed by the social systems and safety nets.

Of course, this has the potential to further feed the entrenched sense of victimization. Nothing has worked for me. There's been no help. Therefore, nothing will ever work for me. There will never be any help. This attitude is understandable, but not insurmountable. Everyday, people find the help they need (or it finds them), or the strength to finally pull themselves (as the cliché says) up by their own bootstraps.

But there are those for whom there is a satisfying payoff in being victims. It may provide emotional gratification. Or it may be in the discomfort it causes others. The reward is in never having to accept responsibility for themselves and their situations. Someone else caused it. Someone else has to fix it. It's their due. They are owed. Their victimhood makes them special.

This type of victimization is shameful and lazy and, ultimately self-sabotaging. People grow weary of pouring help into a bottomless pit of unappreciative and demanding Need. They leave, and the victim is on his or her own again, until he can find the next set of caring, unsuspecting "friends" to suck dry.

My hope is that you are not one of these. In fact, if you've read this far, I doubt that you are a career victim.

What I will be asking you to do is to look honestly at your issues, one at a time. Really face them. It is not hard to do, if you tackle them in small bites. This isn't well-meaning, therapist feel-good fantasy. I did this. Let me repeat: I. Did. This. And so can you. Everything I write here has been put into practice, beginning with the laboratory of Me. The payoff for you is freedom from the past and living a life that is whole, healthy, and healed.

I wanted more for myself than I saw my parents and siblings had. I wanted to be free of it, to be happy, healthy, loved, and to pursue my dreams and have a shot at making them happen.

What do you want for yourself? Make your own list. What are your dreams? Dare to dream them.

The tools offered in this book are ones that I use for myself, and are used by my clients, both adults and children. They are here because they work.

But first let's get educated about what you must do battle

with. Be brave, be honest, and stay calm. Take a break when you need to. You don't have to reinvent the wheel to do this. The wheel is in your hands right now, and I've even paved a road for you.

For the past eleven years I have been working at a treatment center for children who have trauma, abuse, and neglect-related issues. I am their pottery teacher and their massage therapist. Through research and practice, I have been allowed to apply much of what I have learned and experienced to the healing of these children. There have been some failures. There have been more successes.

I know a few things about recovery from abuse and trauma. It has been my journey; living it, studying it, healing it, and working with it. My goal here is to help you make sense of it, so that you can find your own way home. This book is for all my sisters and brothers who share such a history as mine.

Part 1

What You Need To Be Aware Of. Some Terms. Some Definitions.

This book is not going to be an easy read because there are some very predictable reactions that occur in discussions of trauma and abuse. You should be aware of it up front. Otherwise you may put this book down and never look at it again.

It took me years to write this because I have the same reaction to trauma (abuse is trauma) as everyone else. There is a selection of possible responses that can be cycled through repeatedly.

Disassociation (Part 1)

I have walked away from this project several times because of the unpleasantness of the subject. This is an example of *disassociation*. The scope of the project begins to seem so vast that I begin to feel hopeless, which then instigates an additional feeling of helplessness. This can, and has, made me disassociate. During the process of writing and re-writing this book, I sometimes cycled through disassociation, helplessness, and hopelessness, several times a day.

Helplessness, hopelessness, and disassociation are universal responses to trauma and abuse. Because we feel helpless in changing a situation, it becomes a hopeless condition. The best we come to believe we can do is to ignore it. The worst is to attempt to numb the pain, psychologically or with self-medicating chemical assistance. For some of us this may be the only answer to the question, what else can we do?

There are any number of simplistic, made-for-television, sound bite answers available for this; man-up; just do it; just say no. There are kernels of truth in these flippant responses, but the same can be said about most bumper stickers. For our most basic purpose we will take these as meaning to bravely face your experiences, force yourself to stay present to the task and focused on the work you need to perform, including doing the inner work required to understand and heal your damage. You have to massage the scar tissue of your wounds. Avoidance will not help. Refuse to give in to the helplessness and hopelessness you believe is the only response you have available.

That is how I wrote this book.

The difference between you and me is, you have a book now. You aren't going it alone. You don't have to reinvent the wheel.

Triggers

If you have trauma from an event or PTSD (Post Traumatic Stress Disorder), which is a constant physical as well as mental and emotional reaction to trauma, from a single or series of events, your responses can be triggered by anything that reminds you of that event. This can be conscious or unconscious associations or memories. The classic war vet who reacts to loud, explosive noises is an example of a trigger in action. It can also be a touch, a sight, smell, or a taste. Depending upon your history, anything can be a trigger. Some individuals, including myself, can have several triggers.

The worst response to being triggered is the complete flashback, where you are reliving an event in mind and body, just as when it actually occurred. This one is particularly hellish.

Other responses to being triggered are feelings that overwhelm, like a poisonous cloud that seemingly comes from nowhere and stains everything. You are no longer perceiving reality as it is (or was, before you were triggered). You are likely fearful or reactionary. It is possible to remain in triggered states for prolonged periods of time, and even permanently. You can tell you have been triggered when you relive the original feelings and sensations of the event in some manner, and you disassociate.

A key to learning to deal with the results of your triggers is to identify what your triggers are.

Disassociation (Part 2)

Disassociation can occur in response to a triggering event, which causes a traumatic incident to be re-experienced by the individual. He loses touch, or is otherwise no longer present in the moment. He is mentally somewhere else, like in a daydream loaded with anxiety.

Disassociation is a variation of the organism's *Freeze Response*, one of the physical and psychological reactions to a stressor (more on these later). The Freeze Response is a semi-catatonic state that helps reduce pain and suffering caused by insurmountable danger, like a rabbit caught by a hawk. If you have PTSD your nervous system has had a constant flow of adrenalin, so that at times any perceived danger, real or imaginary, can cause you to lock up or otherwise cease to be in the present moment.

It feels as if you are observing you, your life, and the situation around you like it is all happening to someone else. You are simply no longer present in the moment. It's hard to make eye contact or to remain involved in what is going on with or around you.

When any of this happens to you, you have to gently bring yourself back to the present. Then you need to step away from the source of your distress and calm down or de-escalate your emotions. Look at what was going on immediately before you were triggered or disassociated. That action or activity is your trigger.

Knowing this brings you one step closer to self-mastery. And self-mastery is where your healing begins.

Part 2

PTSD (Post Traumatic Stress Disorder) and Some of Its Byproducts

Abuse and trauma can cause boundaries to shrink in, and damage the sense of safety and self. *Boundaries* are those emotional and physical zones (sometimes referred to as *personal space*) that provide us with a protective padding from the mindless dings and fender benders of life in any culture. For the average person, a failure or trespass of a boundary might result in hurt feelings. For the abused and traumatized, the same thoughtless or intentional cruelty can ignite the survival instinct into a wildfire. Their sense of safety and self is threatened. The focus becomes survival.

(Dr. Robert Scaer discusses this at length in his book, *The Body Bears the Burden*.)

Survival is a biological, primitive, animal-like instinct hardwired into our brains and bodies, just as it is with all other species of animals. We are all bound by the same biological rules. Anything that provokes primal fear in you (fear for your life) has the ability to traumatize you. And some animals can literally be scared to death.

For humans, trauma takes a selection of types, shapes, scale, and degrees. We will explore some of these as we progress, but some examples are as large and wide-ranging as *social trauma*, which might be local or global events that horrify us collectively. Remember how 9/11 stunned the world in shock and terror, then how we still feel, a decade or more later. Or the more recent earthquake and tsunami disaster in Japan. These are events with the power to imprint trauma on almost every human living at the time of their occurrences. We might still flinch when an airliner passes over a little too low. We look warily at the cooling towers of the nuclear power plants that might provide our local electricity. Are even the residents of Los Angeles now blasé enough to ignore tremblers that, a year ago, wouldn't rate a comment? I suspect there are now butterflies in stomachs where before there was complacence.

At the other end of the scale are more personal traumas that any of us will encounter in the course of our lives. We can have our *medical traumas*, like surgeries. There are health issues, especially unexpected diagnoses. Who can take a diagnosis of cancer in stride? There are our accidents. And then, infinitely more intimate, are *your* rape, or *your* torture, or *your* abuse.

Somewhere in between these two extremes is *vicarious trauma*, where observing or hearing about someone else's suffering can impact you almost as severely. Or, from another angle, if you have been traumatized it is likely that the people who love you have also been traumatized by your experience or the effect it has had on you. This is beyond empathy. The pain they feel is as authentic as that which you have. Trauma may not be a disease or virus, but it is contagious.

Fight, Flight, or Freeze

A few pages back I mentioned the Freeze Response. This is one of three recognized survival reactions that animals, including humans, have to life-threatening situations. The other two are *Fight* and *Flight*. All are exactly what their names imply. All are automatic responses selected by the body, with little or no conscious thought involved, not much different from an eye blink.

Therefore, if a threat arises for which the Fight Response is both appropriate and available, we will battle with every iota of energy we possess. (Effectiveness is not a consideration at this point.) A fish on a hook does not stop fighting until it is completely exhausted.

Or we might attempt to flee (Flight), put as much distance between the threat and us as we can as fast as we can. Rabbits outrun foxes every day.

But if the situation is so extreme or alien to our experience that neither of these options is available, we can freeze. Deer-in-headlights illustrates this as succinctly as any other example.

What Fight, Flight, and Freeze have in common is that they are not consciously chosen, whether you are a rabbit or a human. These responses are selected by the primal part of the brain automatically and instantly.

Unfortunately, one of the vagaries of our biological or chemical makeup is that all it can take to wipe one of these options from your behavioral menu of responses is a single instance of failure. Think of it as Shock and Awe that actually shocks and awes the particular response out of existence. This is because, based on that single failure, the primal part of your brain may deem it to be ineffective, and erase it. This is not a conscious process. You do not think, "This didn't work, so I won't ever try it again." It is an automatic delete.

(Special note: The computer analogy might be more accurate in most cases. It is extremely difficult to actually fully delete or erase data from a hard drive. In most cases, deleting only removes the labels from the data that allows the computer to find it. The data itself is still there, and can be recovered. Your erased Responses behave similarly.)

An important characteristic found in Fight or Flight conditions is that the energy or charge generated within the nervous system is depleted or burned off. In the animal world the aftereffects - the energy generated in the nervous system - of the Freeze Response can be expelled, if the animal survives the incident. In their natural environment, the stressors of being prey seldom traumatize even the most vulnerable animals. They have a built-in coping mechanism that, for cultural, social, or environmental reasons, we humans either no longer have or have rejected.

Animal survivors "shake it off." The twitching and rippling of the hide and skin, or the kicking of the paws or hooves, is the residual nervous energy being discharged from the nervous system. The incident is over. The danger has passed. The animal is not wounded, and is no worse off than it was before. The zebras return to their grazing while lions devour another, just a few yards away. Everything is as it should be.

We rarely do that. When we "survive" a physical or psychological incident, we are nonetheless damaged by it because we do not follow through by shaking it off - discharging the nervous energy generated by the Freeze Response. By not releasing this energy we do damage to our nervous systems. Fight and Flight burn of the energy generated in the nervous system.

Of course, even animals, under some circumstances (such as captivity), cannot sustain the resiliency required for complete recovery after repeated assaults. And we, like them, can become constantly on guard. In the mental health field this is called "hypervigilance." Or we (and they) "numb out." We disassociate or freeze.

Your genetic makeup, what you inherited from your parents and close ancestors, determines the strength of your nervous system. (This is sometimes described as "nerves of steel" or a "nervous disposition.") This is a contributing, but not limiting, factor to how many traumas you can experience before you develop Post Traumatic Stress Disorder.

Both adults and children can develop PTSD. For some, one incident is enough to create a lifelong psychological wound. For others, it may take multiple assaults. Children are particularly vulnerable because their nervous systems are still developing.

PTSD can literally rewire the brain and change the way it works.

In the case of a child, if the abuse or trauma occurred before the child learned to speak, he or she will still carry the memory of the experience and the feelings it caused in them, but will not have the words to express or relate them. They are at the *preverbal* stage of their development. What they do manage to express will be in a crude manner because they have no coping skills and no other way to communicate. Withdrawal, hindered development, and acting out or some of the behaviors through which a child may attempt to communicate his distress and pain.

PTSD is as physical as it is mental and emotional.

Trauma releases intense amounts of hormones in your body. Repeated traumas, or even just one big one, can destroy the switching mechanism that controls the stress hormones. This switch is the HPA; the *Hypothalamus, Pituitary, Adrenal axis* or complex. The main hormones involved are *cortisol* and *adrenaline* (epinephrine; also a neurotransmitter). Both are produced by the adrenal glands, and both serve complicated biological purposes. Too much of either has negative effects on the body and mind.

Chronic stress or PTSD will excite prolonged production of these hormones. This has a multitude of detrimental impacts on the body, including a host of inflammatory diseases. Your body breaks down, like a car driven to hard and fast for too long with no stops for maintenance. Also, as you may have noticed, your nerves will always be on edge.

This was a simplified description of your body's response to trauma. Does it sound familiar to you?

The good news is that there is a cure, and it is briefer than the description of the problem. We call it *"self-regulation."* Your experience tells you that your body can no longer calm down on its own. However, you can learn to control this. I am here to help you learn the techniques you need.

Memorize this:

Your body is an incredible self-healing mechanism, with a beyond-brilliant design. It is designed to adapt to almost any environment and it will, if given the right encouragement. With proper care and time, you can mend much of the damage, just like any wound.

The first key is to do your best to avoid further trauma.

Adrenal Fatigue

It bears mentioning that adrenal fatigue shares many of the same pathologies of PTSD in its effect upon the body. Unfortunately, at this writing there are no insurance codes related to this ailment. In the logic of corporate insurance companies and their relationships with medical practitioners, if there is not a code for an ailment, it cannot be treated and billed to the policy.

Therefore, by this logic, adrenal fatigue does not exist. And since it doesn't exist, it isn't being treated. We are stuck with an imaginary affliction that no one has to do anything about.

Fortunately, there are excellent books available on the subject that offers excellent suggestions on how to manage the problem on your own. One of the most helpful I found is *Adrenal Fatigue: the 21st Century Stress Syndrome* by James L. Wilson. And there are a growing number of doctors arguing for its recognition as a legitimate affliction.

Retraumatization

If the traumatic experience was too severe or horrifying, your brain may not be able to put it into context. Because you are unable to make sense of it or put it in the past it can remain free-floating and be ever-present. Or it can get buried in the subconscious or unconscious mind, and you may unconsciously attract or re-create a similar situation in an attempt to master the trauma. This is not a conscious choice. It happens because there was no resolution to the situation. With or without your cooperation, the mind needs to make sense of it, master it, and put it in the past.

You have to consciously and willfully work through your

trauma to truly be free of it.

Re-education

The body, mind, and spirit are one. You are a whole being. But the way we think about the body in Western culture is not as a unified whole. We have different doctors - "specialists" - for our kidneys, lungs, hearts, and our bones. This view sees us as fragmented machines and sustains the illusion that we are not whole and unified beings.

Nothing could be further from reality.

If you have been traumatized, your recovery hinges on the importance of thinking of yourself as a whole person. Recovery requires you to work with your body, mind, and spirit, sometimes simultaneously. Yet trauma can literally shatter this unity, causing divisions between any two or all three elements.

Muscle Memory

The body has what is called *muscle memory*. This may mean slightly different things depending on the physiological context it is used in. For example, the repetition of a function-specific motion - practice - gave Tiger Woods his phenomenal golf swing. A bodybuilder bench-presses his bar through the same plane of motion. These actions "educate" the particular muscles to the required activity, so that they come to "know" what to expect. This even makes piano playing and touch-typing possible. The body remembers, and remembering, is able to excel.

For our purposes, the body remembers everything that has ever happened to it.

When a muscle has been injured badly enough through accident or other everyday trauma, it can "forget" its job or function. (This is one aspect of learned helplessness.) The physical therapy prescribed is to help re-educate or re-train it on how to do its job.

When hit, your muscle forms a bruise, your body responds by releasing stress hormones, your mind responds by being hyperalert or forgetful, your energy responds by drawing inward, and ultimately your spirit can lose a bit of itself and its sense of safety in the world.

Sadly, some of us have never had a sense of being safe in the world.

Your response to trauma must be to choose to relearn how to live and reclaim a sense of safety, even if it is for the first time.

Learned Helplessness

Just like your muscles can forget a trained function, you can develop *learned helplessness* as a result of trauma.

Learned helplessness is anything that you were once able to do, but then lost faith or confidence in your ability to perform accurately or safely. This may be paying your bills or getting a job. It also includes being happy, recovering, and taking back control over your life. It goes hand-in-hand with the helplessness and hopelessness linked to disassociation and the degradation of your personal boundaries.

You have to dare to live your life again, differently from what you currently have, perhaps even differently from what you had before. A first step is to manage your responsibilities, even if they seem overwhelming at first. This is the beginning of reclaiming yourself for you. You might be all you have right now. But you have to dare to be your own hero, because good heroes are not always there when we need them.

Part 3

Pathways in the Brain

Neural pathways begin to form in the brain at birth, and perhaps even in utero. (Some experts argue that what the fetus experiences in the womb influences cognitive and emotional development of the child.) Food is good, being wet is bad, hopefully we are wanted and loved. We both feel and learn these things as part of growth and development. This is our pathways forming.

These neural pathways are the wiring of your brain that your thoughts, ideas, feelings, and other processes move along, just like electricity. Your interactions with the outer world, how your parents relate to you, what you learn and think, cause this wiring to grow and expand throughout your brain. Most of this growth took place in your first three years. By the time you were five, most of your basic wiring had been established.

We have beliefs and ideas about who we are because of the messages we have been given from our beginnings. This includes our value, or lack of, in our families. In our first few years, most of what we learn is non-verbal. We learn by observing and experiencing our parents (or other caregivers), siblings, and the world immediately around us.

So let's say that you are growing up and the messages you are given are negative: You are useless; you are no good; you are stupid, bad, fill-in-the-blank. These are the messages that build your pathways, your interior responses. The more of these messages you receive, the deeper and more ingrained these negative pathways and responses become. It does not matter how untrue they are. In your subconscious, you are what you are told you are.

When I was growing up, almost all I heard from my father

was that I was stupid, a useless piece of shit, and that I would never amount to anything. From almost the beginning these messages became the well-worn pathways my brain and mind always went down in moments of stress. They promised to become the self-fulfilling prophecies. But I learned to cut the flow of them before they destroyed me completely. Call it "reprogramming" if you want. I'm proof that it can be done, that it works, and that you can do it on your own.

This is part of what helped to save me.

Before I started to become my own person (growth), my mother loved me. I was cute and fun to dress up. Equally important, my maternal grandparents lived nearby. They truly loved my siblings and me. Even so, this could not stop the degrading messages given us by our father. Even when I was pre-verbal the abuse he heaped upon my older brother made an impression upon me.

It became my turn as I grew, thus imprinting negativity - by example - in my younger sister. My mother couldn't help us. Right or wrong, she was more interested in saving herself. So I could not turn to or trust her.

Fortunately, I was (and am) contrary by nature. This, of course, simply gave additional cause to any abuse my father justified. But it meant that I would not let his negative messages (stupid, useless) be my absolute truth. Even after the most extreme insults I would, in my childish wisdom, chant to myself that it wasn't true. I wasn't stupid. I wasn't useless.

Those negative pathways still formed, of course. I was young and had few defenses against them. But I also had those few positive pathways, grown from when there was no reason to question my mother's love for me. And the love and belonging that came from my grandparents made a core part of me strong, healthy, and whole.

But this was just me. Your circumstance may seem to be radically different. You didn't have those grandparents. Your mother never showed any love for you. You didn't have anything like that. So nothing I offer can apply to you.

Sorry, but I don't accept that. Just because you did not have the little bit of basic affection to start off with doesn't mean that you did not have something you can draw on now. Somewhere in your past and experiences there is something so positive that no amount of trauma and abuse has managed to destroy it. Your job, whether you want it or not, is to find that precious gem and build on it.

Here is the good part: Pathways are actually easy to change. It takes vigilance, the will to, and lots of repetition, just like using muscle memory to learn to play guitar or anything else. You build the memory of something different. Think of it as building a new road that goes someplace you want to be inside yourself.

If you are tired of being your own abuser - and you *should* be - give this a try.

Affirmations

First, figure out what negative messages you received about yourself. One clue may be to see where your mind goes when something goes wrong in your life. What do you tell yourself about who you are? Pay attention to these moments and use them to start your list.

Next, go down that list and think of a positive message to replace each negative one. Then every time the old message pops up or is triggered, actively replace it with the new one.

For me, the easiest way to do this was to stop all negative thought and self-talk. No more "I'm stupid" or "I'll never amount to anything." These became "I just learned something new" and "I worked my way through massage school." In the light of these truths, how could the lies that had been beat into me hold up? I traced them to their roots - my father - and banished them from my mind.

The new messages are usually called *affirmations*. These

positive thoughts yield a healthier mind. I found that the pathways change quickly once I cut off their flow and rerouted them. Sometimes it only took a matter of days. I would get real serious about them and target them one at a time, starting with the most critical beliefs.

And if it takes longer, so what? There are studies that indicate a behavior or programming can be changed in twenty-one days, if the individual is diligent in her replacement behavior or affirmations.

To do affirmations properly, you must make every effort to believe and feel them to be true. Fake it until you feel it.

Don't think this is silly. Odds are, you've talked yourself into incorrect attitudes before. Why not try to do the same thing, but with a healthier purpose in mind? If it helps, think of it as acting. Everyone wants to be a movie star. In this case, you are the star, writer, and director.

Most important, you belong to the school of acting called "method." Method actors immerse themselves so deeply into their characters that their true personalities do not resurface for the duration of the play or filming. They might even acquire the skills associated with the character. Robert De Niro, for example, learned to play the saxophone for a role. Robin Williams learned to speak Russian *and* play the sax. And Ewan McGregor wondered if you should actually try the heroin his character was addicted to.

These are extreme examples. You certainly don't need to carry your affirmations that far (especially heroin). But they show the power that these actors have in their minds to make faking it real, not only to us, but to them.

You and your mind have that exact same power to the exact same degree. You can use it to learn to play the saxophone if you want. But first, use it to heal yourself.

New thoughts freshen the mind. I am a very visual person, so picturing my new truth was very helpful. This built new pathways.

Likewise, every time you learn something new you are developing your own new pathways in your brain. People who continue to learn and grow throughout their lifetimes stay young in ways that time cannot steal. It keeps the brain healthy.

The Conscious and Subconscious Mind

The conscious part of the brain is fairly self-explanatory. It is our awareness of the world, our place in it, our interactions and our experience of reality.

The conscious/subconscious mind interaction is a two-way street. Your subconscious influences your actions and awareness; so, too, can you use your conscious mind to re-create or modify your subconscious. You can build new neural pathways and work on existing ones to lay a solid foundation in life. You can learn new things. Even if you can't go to school, libraries and the Internet make books and information more readily available to you than at any other time in history.

My grandfather was a self-educated man, and I am largely self-educated. Ultimately, it doesn't matter where your education comes from. Either you know something, or you don't. When a new subject interests me I will find everything available on it, weighing the various research, debates, and data against each other. I know my education on a matter is nearing completion when the available information ceases to yield any new ideas and begins to repeat itself. Then I synthesize my own hypothesis - if I need to carry it that far - and move on.

A college degree is a wonderful life accomplishment. But it is out of reach for too many of us. Even so, this is not an excuse for a sedentary mind. A childhood history of abuse may have stunted some of your development. You may have social, emotional, and intellectual challenges resulting from this. You couldn't finish high school. You never got your GED. College or advanced courses would be a joke. Is this what you believe?

Why?

You can change that simply by believing in something different. As I said, you have talked yourself into foolish beliefs about yourself before. Now talk yourself into smart ones. Something like - for instance - determining to get your GED would be a good place to start. It would be good practice in self-discipline. And having a goal to keep in sight provides you with a tangible marker.

The point is, you tell yourself this is something you are going to do. Then you tell yourself you are going to keep working at it until it is done. And then you congratulate yourself for doing it successfully.

You've learned something new. You're no longer "stupid," and, more importantly, you can't call yourself stupid anymore.

You've changed a pathway.

That was just one simple example. Your situation is probably radically different. But just because it is, just because I don't mention your specific history or issue, it does not mean you can't do something similar to make the change in your life that you need.

Just don't be afraid to learn what you don't know. Make the effort to figure out what that is.

The first few times you try something new, you're probably not going to be very good at it. No one is. You have to build the new pathways and the muscle memory of having done or studied a thing dozens or hundreds of times. That is where all learning starts. Repetition, repetition, repetition.

Most adults have an aversion to failure and a fear of looking foolish, even those without our backgrounds. The fact is, failure happens. So does looking foolish, whether or not the video shows up on YouTube. Both happen to even the most successful. And, unless they are seriously maladjusted and true threats to society, they don't care. They take it in stride. And so can you. Even just the attempt can be its own reward. Applaud your own bravery. And keep at it until you experience the satisfaction of having learned something new. It far outweighs any embarrassment your earlier attempts may have made you suffer.

I taught myself most of the art I create. In the process I learned a lot about what doesn't work and even more about what does. One of the results is that my art is distinctively my own, recognizable as unique pieces.

In particular I learned pottery largely on my own. Now I teach it. I give my students just enough of the basics to keep them from having to "re-invent the wheel." Then I get out of the way and see what happens. I am often amazed at the incredible things people create once they have those basics. I have witnessed genius at work in so many, and that is so beautiful to behold.

Yes, there are limitations. You can't become a medical doctor this way, or an airline pilot. And if you tried, I would not want to be either your patient or your passenger. But jailhouse lawyers, self-educated in prison libraries, have changed the course of the criminal justice system. And there are handymen, cooks, dancers, artists, writers, and an endless list of achievements and education gained by people just like us who have taught themselves.

The world is your playground. Take classes or go to school if you can. If you can't, learn on your own what you want to know. Passion and practice make for success, and success makes for improved self-esteem.

Don't be ashamed at being a beginner at anything. Everything accomplished in life by anyone starts this way.

To learn silversmithing and stonecutting, I served a three-year apprenticeship in a rock shop. I worked for free (my tuition), and acquired the education, skills, and knowledge I wanted for the same price (labor). Not only was it fulfilling to achieve a goal I set for myself, I had a great time doing it. I did not learn everything there is to know about making jewelry, but the pieces I crafted at the end demonstrated how far I had come when compared to my awkward first attempts. Like my first pots, they might have been a little embarrassing - "failures" because they weren't the perfection I envisioned.

But after repetition, repetition, repetition, I have produced artful, meticulous pieces my clients and friends prize.

So take classes or read on your own, become a student to someone who knows something about anything that interests you, join a writer's group or take music lessons. Have the courage to let yourself be guided.

The Subconscious Mind

The *subconscious mind*, as the name suggests, is what lies beneath our everyday awareness. Your subconscious stores massive amounts of information, more than any computer yet built. Scenes from movies, words to songs you loved twenty years ago, a face above your cradle. . . every detail of your every experience resides there. It is what is accessed by hypnosis or suggestion.

It is also the place your dreams come from. Dream interpretation is one way to get to know your subconscious. The symbols that come up in your dreams mean something. It is your quiet, hidden, suppressed self trying to communicate buried thoughts and feelings with your waking self, even if only to warn against eating buffalo wings and green chili in the same meal.

Carl Jung believed, as do I, that we share in a *collective unconscious*, generated by our experiences as human beings across the generations. Therefore, some symbols are universal. That means that, in context, a select number of symbols represent the same thing or things to almost every human, regardless of the culture or background. More often though, the evolution of time, the introduction of new artifacts into culture and society, and the differences between cultures has caused meanings to diverge.

Regardless, look at the objects that crop up in your dreams; dogs, horses, helicopters, fire, or whatever. Question what they represent to you, and question the dream situation they appeared in. If this is daunting, there are many books on dream interpretation available. I prefer editions that detail what a symbol meant throughout human history in all cultures. I will often feel the correctness of how it applies to my particular dream when I read it. This comes from experience, which is the same thing as repetition, repetition, repetition.

My most important point is that the subconscious mind is a driving force that is dangerous to ignore. Remember retraumatization? Your very dreams can reenact your original trauma with the same result. It is a malleable and valuable part of the brain that, connected to PTSD, can make your life hell. But it is also a part that you can learn to control. Your subconscious is very much liken that old dictary maxim, "You are what you eat." Your subconscious believes *anything* you feed it. If you put fear and trauma into it, that is what it is going to leak out into your conscious life.

The subconscious mind believes everything. It does not have the discernment between truth and lie, real and unreal, that the conscious mind has. It does not have the filters. This is how people under hypnosis can be convinced to do silly things, like the classic Cluck-Like-A-Chicken carnival routine.

The quickest and easiest way for you to access that part of your brain is during the minutes right before you go to sleep, or in the free-floating, uncertain minutes as you awaken. Your conscious mind is less likely to interfere with your plans in these periods. This is where you begin to retake control of your past.

Meditation is another technique you can use, and can be more active and deliberate, as you choose the time you perform it. In fact, meditation might be one of the most important tools you can add to your psychological "medicine chest."

Years ago, I had a book which I loaned out and never saw again. Unfortunately, I cannot recall for certainty the title or the names of the authors, but it might have been from Richard Bandler and John Grinder, the founders of Neuro-Linguistic

Programming (NLP). The essence of their premise was that we can approach our subconscious mind with the intent of deliberately rewriting our personal histories. Not only is this possible, but this action will change the impact past trauma has upon us.

It is far simpler in practice than it sounds in explanation. I know because I did it. It worked for me in some deep ways.

In brief, here is how to do it.

If you are practiced at meditation, get into a meditative state. Otherwise, do this as you prepare for sleep, or upon awakening. A little warning; some of this might be painful at first.

Close your eyes and relax deeply. Recall the first event that ever damaged you. Try to remember every detail, even the most terrible ones, if you are up to it. If this takes more strength than you currently have, "edit" the memory like an R-rated movie shown on broadcast television. "Bleep" the language for now. You can "watch" the unedited version later, when you feel stronger, and know what is hiding in the closet.

Now imagine how you wish you had handled the situation. Was there something you could have said that would have defused the moment? Say it now. Would it have taken more? Then give yourself that more. Vividly imagine yourself fighting back or escaping, or whatever would have resolved the situation in your favor. Then focus on how you wish it had been. *Create a new memory*. Imagine every detail of this new, happy image, including how it feels. Be with it. Tell yourself that this is your truth, and don't resist with logic. Just let it be your new truth.

Now take a break, or move on to the next issue. You will be going through every traumatic issue in your history in this way. Sometimes you will have to repeat the process, especially if you had to edit the memory. But you will improve with practice.

I cannot and will not tell you that this tactic will cure

everything. But it sure lightens the load. The weight of your past can be reduced until it is manageable.

Because the subconscious mind lacks filters and firewalls, and believes everything it is exposed to, I take special care in what finds the door into it. I don't watch movies featuring violence or horror, and I don't read books from these genres. The only exception is the news on television and newspapers. But not always. If I sense that what I am about to watch or read might be a trigger for my own past issues, I stop. If it is something I should know, someone will give me an abridged version, minus the worst details.

I monitor myself, especially if I am having a hard time with world events, or already think that the human race is doomed. I don't add to that by inviting even more disturbing stories in. Short and effective countermeasures are to seek out the opposite. A good, or even bad, comedy can stifle my darkest moods, even if only for a little while. This can buy me the time I need to gather the positive energy I need to oppose the negative forces outside.

Our thoughts do shape our reality, both conscious and unconscious. Make the effort to work with them.

There have been countless books written about how thoughts shape reality. For the world outside us almost everything you see, touch, taste, and feel in a day first began as a thought inside someone's mind. These ideas shaped their inner realities until they were finally expressed in the outer, physical world.

The healing of your inner world begins the same way. You have the idea to heal. So work on the wiring. Form new pathways. Be selective about what you let impact your subconscious, and guard against the negative and damaging until you are stronger.

Some realities may be too awful for you to consciously face, but your subconscious knows all of them, and much may hide in it that, even ignored, impact you and your actions.

Regardless, recovery requires you to be mindful of both the conscious and unconscious activities of your brain.

Meditation is very healthy for the mind and brain. It turns down the constant chatter and the eternal inner dialogue of the mind, and just lets us be with our quieter, subconscious mind. It eases the pressures on the nervous system and calms the body, mind, and spirit. Meditation is a healer of the whole being.

Go ahead and make fun of affirmations. Everyone does. But after you finish laughing (which is a curative, too), give them a serious try. They are very helpful tools. If you have been abused, it is vital to your recovery to replace negative messages with positive ones. Believe the best in yourself. For that matter, believe the best in others, too. Doing the one usually encourages the other.

Breathing

If you already practice meditation, then you probably know the technique and benefits of *hu gong breathing*. (It might also be called *yoga breathing*.) And if you have never heard of it, do not worry. This isn't kung fu. This is breathing, pure and simple. You already do it without thinking. Now you want to do it with awareness and focus.

Sit or lie down and relax. Take in as much air as your lungs can hold, then hold it there for about five seconds. Don't strain. Just exhale. Then do it again. Most important, pay attention to the action of your breathing. Feel the air enter and fill your chest, and feel it leave. Focus on this.

Practice this for as long as you can, even if you can only rob a few minutes from your day in the beginning. But make the time. This is more important for you than who gets voted off the island or kicked off the dance show. Once you get into it you will easily increase the time you devote to it, and not even know it.

I like to hu gong breathe twenty minutes or so a day. I just breathe and sit quietly in silence. I use it to calm down and focus, and some other things we will get into later.

Being

Just sit or lie down. Don't think about everything that isn't getting done. Don't do anything. Just *be* for ten minutes. Push away any thoughts that don't have anything to do with your breathing. Try listening to soft music and let each note go through your energy, each taking a bit of your burden as it goes. Even if you do nothing else, learning to just be quiet with yourself will give your nervous system a break from tensions.

Meditation is simply going deeper and deeper into the silence.

The Mini Vacation

I am fortunate to be a Colorado girl, but I also love Montana and Wyoming. I have lived in all three states, and I simply love the mountains. So when I need a getaway when I can't actually get away I imagine a beautiful pine-laced path, and I start walking. I breathe in the scented air, feel the breeze in my hair, and the sun warm my shoulders. I listen to the birds and the trees, and I feel the peace they contribute to the world.

I keep walking until I come to a meadow full of bright wildflowers. I cross the meadow, following the whisper of a stream. I listen to the water and watch the sunlight wink off the ripples of the water. Sometimes there is a large, sun-warmed rock on the bank. I lie on it and watch the clouds . . .

I use this if I have trouble sleeping, or just need a break from the hectic pace of my day. Look into yourself and find the similar sort of environment that relaxes you. Then take that little vacation, and calm your being.

Your Relationship With Yourself

Before you can have healthy connections with anyone else, you have to foster and build a healthy relationship with yourself. We all have traits in our natures that challenge us, as well as positive traits that make us lovable and unique.

How would you relate to your best friend if they had your issues? You should give yourself no less. Truly be kind to yourself, like you would be to someone you love. This is how you should relate to yourself, problems and all. *You are not the enemy*. What originally impacted you is.

Trauma often brings with it guilt, shame, and regret. Set those aside for now. You'll get to them, one at a time.

The circumstances of my life have led me to say and do things that were awful for me and the people around me. Survival mode changes people. When you are forced to react by instinct you are not capable of thought. When we feel threatened we resort to the automatic responses of Fight, Flight, or Freeze. That is how the universe has designed us.

And, as with so much else, the universe can be politically incorrect. Men are more prone to the Fight Response than the other two. Women and children tend to Flight and Freeze. That's how nature works.

Happily, one of the things that makes us human is our ability to learn to make choices that defy programming.

(In the context of this discussion, if you are a woman, then you quite likely have a long-term experience with the Freeze response.)

When I think about my regrets I think about all the circumstances surrounding the situation and my actions in response to it. This may also mean my inaction. I ask myself if I did the best I could with what I had to work with.

This requires me to be completely honest with myself. It can be more difficult to be honest with ourselves than with others, but the work we are doing requires it. Lie all you need to the rest of the world, but your own healing demands that you tell yourself the truth. Like a medical doctor, if you don't know what is truly wrong, you can't fix it.

If I determine that I did the best that I could, then the issue is little more than an unfortunate incident. It is not my fault. I can let go of the regret and the shame, and learn from the mistake that put me in that situation in the first place.

Of course, it is not always this simple. Some small issues may resolve so easily, while others are too large or devastating to be addressed by a single dismissal. I have made a few decisions in my life that have been so weighted that I have had to repeatedly analyze the choice I made. Walking away from my family is one of these, as it should be. I did not want to lose that. But every time I thought the problems weren't as large as I remembered them to be, or softened because I wanted and needed something to call "family," I ended up sucked back into the same toxic drama.

It is still the right choice for me.

And if I didn't do the best I could, then I still have work to do. Sometimes, as detailed before, this requires revisiting the situation and exploring other options. Other times I find some act of restitution I can perform. This cannot always include the original cast of characters. But someone in need will benefit.

This helps keep my relationship with myself healthy and honest, and can for you, too. It may take practice, and you may have a few false starts or well-intentioned atonements go awry, but the more you do, the better you get.

Repetition, repetition, repetition.

Attempt the same techniques to deal with shame and guilt. If you have a debt, find a way to pay it back to someone who needs it. If you don't owe for that, then let it go.

I weigh my choices with care, choose my words with

sensitivity, and select my responses to situations with thoughtfulness to not add the burdens of more guilt, shame, or regret to my soul, or to the troubles others already carry.

The Body-Mind Connection

As was previously detailed, the body remembers everything that has ever happened to it. Have you ever tried to touch someone's face, only to have them flinch? That could be the muscle memory of being slapped.

Likewise, every cell in your body has a nucleus. The nucleus is, essentially, the "brain" of the cell. It knows what it is and what it is supposed to do. It also has a memory of everything it has experienced. It is possible that it even passes this information down to the next generation of cells.

Your *affect* (feeling or emotion) is what you carry around with you and present to the world. It is your overall energy. It is the energy that surrounds you, what might also be called your *aura*. If you have suffered trauma and abuse it is in your *energy/aura*. It has been my experience that torture and sexual abuse or trauma are two of the most damaging affects to a person's energy. They injure the aura in some, and shatter it in others.

Before you dismiss my use of "energy" and "aura" as more hippy-dippy, New-Agey twaddle, take a glance at any basic physics book. At the most basic level, all any of us is is pure energy. We are a bunch of molecules that hang out together. Molecules, in turn, are a bunch of atoms that hang out together. And atoms are composed of smaller and ever more exotic components that physicists can only speculate about, and label with invented names. Your FaceBook Friends lists has nothing on what unites your body into one creature.

EEGs (electroencephalograpy) peer into our brains and help diagnose problems by recording and measuring the brain's electrical activity, generated both passively and as a result of active thought ("I think, therefore, I am." René Descartes). This is energy, and one of the most basic laws of physics - thermodynamics, particularly - states that "Energy can neither be created nor destroyed."

In short, the energy (measurable by scientific methods and technologies) that makes us us, is forever.

I call it the soul.

I think in terms of energy. I spent most of my life in the study of metaphysics, the focus of which is, simply put, energy. It was an interest of my grandfather and my mother, so it became an early interest of mine.

It was my original path to God. Metaphysics helped me understand how energy worked. While New Agers, druids, and wiccans follow a similar path, it was not my quest to be one of them. I just wanted to know on my terms, and the more I studied, the more I came to understand in my way, the greater I came to trust what felt like deep truth.

Now, years and decades later, physics is catching up with what I learned, and is proving much of what I believe to be true. Physicists wouldn't admit it, even under waterboarding, but the boundary between "physics" and "metaphysics" is disintegrating. Eventually, the only difference between a hard physicist and someone like me will be that the scientist can do the really hard math.

So, for our purposes here: If you have been repeatedly victimized, it is imprinted in your energy. And what makes the situation worse is that this imprint is like bleeding in shark-infested waters. The sort of predators that victimized you in the first place can identify you with a glance, and it pulls them in. Victims are more vulnerable to predators and victimizers. The woman who continues to attract abusive men as romantic partners, the person who has been molested or raped at different times by different people, all become less able to defend and protect themselves.

Worse, they may even seek out the men or women who

empower themselves through the weakness of their victims. In psychotherapy this is referred to as the *re-creation of trauma.*

In wild nature (or even in your backyard, around your birdbath), the weakest and most vulnerable of the herd are the ones that end up being dinner. Part of the predator's ability to target prey seems to transcend the five senses. Terms like "ESP" and "empathy" carry too much pop culture baggage, so I prefer to call it the *felt sense.*

People and prey-creatures who are adept at hiding vulnerability and weakness as a survival trait are still regularly detected by the hunters. There are often chinks in the armor (aura) of the wounded and weak that leak the condition of the prey to the predator. The predator may not see or scent anything (the five classic senses), but *feels* the weakness, and is thus able to target the prey. The predator has this sense either as instinct or conscious, deliberate training. Humans may explain it by other labels, but all other creatures accept it, and live or die by its abilities.

We all live by the same biological rules. This energy is real. If you disagree, then you have never noticed how the "feeling" of a room changes when someone in a really bad mood comes in and pollutes the atmosphere.

Thinking in terms of energy is the most effective way to deal with trauma in the body. It is essential to recovery.

Try the exercise in the following chapter for a month. If you do nothing else but this for yourself, it will make a noticeable difference in how you feel.

Feeling the Body/Mind

Find a quiet place where you can sit comfortably and not be disturbed.

Yes, I "don't know what" your life is like, or how hard it is to get a minute's peace. Nevertheless, this is something you have to do for yourself. No one else can get that "minute's peace" for you, just like no one else can heal you. This is simply the first thing you have to learn to do for yourself. You are taking responsibility for your healing because you can't count on anyone else to do it for you.

Waking or rising a little earlier each day worked for me. The twenty minutes I lost in sleep was more than made up for by the energy, strength, and calm I gained by doing the following.

So. You are in that quiet place, physically comfortable if not yet relaxed. Take a deep breath and hold it for a count of five, then breathe out. This is the *hu gong breath*. Keep using this technique of breathing through the entire exercise.

As you breathe in, pay attention to your body. Where is it tense? Imagine that the air of your breath goes to one of those spots. For the space of that five-count, let that air dilute the tension. Then, as you exhale, imagine the tension swirling out with your breath. If you feel you have to do this several times, go ahead, but don't focus too long on a single location in the beginning. Likely, you have a number of spots, all clamoring for your attention. Try to bring a few along at a time, until you get the hang of it. But don't spend your entire session just on the physical or psychological aspects of tension. You have other issues and components that are in as much need.

See? You have purged some of your tension. Don't be surprised if this brings emotions of some nature to the surface.

Feelings of anger, fear, grief, shame, and pain often arise. Just as you did with tension, you have to be present to them. Identify them and acknowledge their existence in you. For now you don't need to explore why you are feeling them. Remember, you have only twenty minutes. You just need to know that they are there, and that you have the intention of doing something about them.

As you did with your tense spots, pick one; fear, for example. I have a menu of things I can be afraid of or for, but it can easily be non-specific and ambiguous. It does not matter what the fear is about. To address it, I begin my hu gong breath with the intention of breathing in a sense of calm and safety that I can flood over my fear. Five counts later, I exhale the old air, sending with it not only the carbon dioxide gas we generate as living, oxygen-breathing creatures, but also the poison that is my fear.

And as I do this, I see everything - the incorporeal emotion, the molecules of oxygen, even the cells of my body - as pure energy. Sometimes I picture this energy like the images sent to us from the Hubble Space Telescope. It shows the stuff of us writ large; energy on a grand scale. This allows me to find and release my fear from every particle of my being. I imagine sending this energy to a black hole in the universe that it can't escape from and pollute my environment.

By the way. You have seen me use the word, "intention," several times already. *Intention means that you have a deliberate purpose driving what you are doing.* You want to heal, so you are seeking out ways to make that happen. Your *intention*, then, is to make yourself better by consciously identifying a problem and consciously applying whatever corrections it requires.

Use what comes to you. You have to learn to trust what comes to you, because your answers lie therein. So make that effort to *be* with yourself in that way for those twenty short minutes. This is where you begin to replace every negative thing you release with something positive and supportive.

Don't be overwhelmed by it all. Lots of bad stuff has happened to you. It may be hard to know which cruelty to start with. Don't spend energy prioritizing them at this point. This is where you use what comes to you. And regardless of the size, don't be disappointed that it isn't all fixed at once. Any size bite you take out of a problem is that much less you will have to deal with next time.

And do not worry if nothing comes up, or you can't settle on one issue long enough to do anything with it. Take advantage of the moment to practice the hu gong breathing. When nothing arises for me I just focus on my breath, or I will pray, or I will do some conscious work with my subconscious mind and my body/mind connection. I can let this time be anything it needs to be, because even without an active problem to address I am giving me back to myself.

You need to bring two important aspects of yourself to the table in this meditation process.

The first is the *Observing Self*, the part of you that is detached from physical reality and just watches, not judging or even thinking about an event or an issue. It is an awareness of what is within you.

The other is the *Experiencing Self*. This encompasses the full range of your personal existence. What your body feels, and how. All the emotions and sensations stored within it.

My mind is the *Observer*. Everything else that makes me a unique individual feels the *Experience*.

With these two aspects to work from, I release from my energy/aura whatever comes up for me, neither judging nor analyzing any of it. Later, I - my observing mind - can think it through, if I want to.

To learn to use the Observing Self and the Experiencing Self in this way is profoundly helpful just in everyday existence. To address your deeper issues with this skill arms you with a weapon that can strengthen and protect you for whatever battles you need to fight.

Body workers and psychotherapists agree here:

The only way out of pain is through it.

You can't ignore it or wish it away. It builds on itself. If you try to escape it with any of the easily accessible tools, drink or drugs, you only compound your problems.

Your work is to go into your pain, feel it, and release it. That is all your body and your mind wants, and what recovery demands.

I know what fear or ever terror might be provoked in you by that thought. But look at it this way:

You have already survived it.

What you are doing now is putting the cleanup crew to work to pack it up, tidy the place a bit, and letting it go.

PTSD puts tremendous pressure on the body, mind, and spirit. This technique is an effective way of bleeding it off, so to speak: To begin the process of defrosting the self. If you can't manage twenty minutes, then do ten to start. Or five. But do it every day.

Also, when a person has experienced substantial or prolonged trauma, correct breathing can be a real issue. Breathing tends to become shallow because deep, natural breathing may not be easy or comfortable when you are so full of pain, grief, anger, or so forth. The less you do, the less it seems to hurt.

This is a lie. Breathing is necessary to life. Your body and brain need oxygen to live and function. More profoundly, the act of breathing is about taking life into your self and being.

If you practice the hu gong breath, in time you will begin to breathe deeper and more correctly. By letting go of tensions, stressors, and negative emotions, you free yourself of them and your breathing becomes even more healthful and helpful.

Note: If your issues have occupied your being for any length of time, their absence may leave a void in your heart and mind. It is important that you be prepared to replace the negativity you release with something positive. I do this so that I don't unconsciously attract anything unwelcome or even dangerous to fill that void.

How I Learned To Manage My Emotions (So They Didn't Manage Me) (And Other Helpful Hints)

In the environment I grew up in, expressing feelings was often a dangerous thing. They were a chink in my armor that my abusers could exploit to get inside and do their damage. I learned to suppress and hide them. This is a universal response to an unsafe environment.

It is not uncommon to hide unpleasant feelings from ourselves, ignoring or avoiding them. But it puts more pressure on what may already be a dangerously overloaded system; body, mind, and spirit. Nothing goes away if you ignore it.

I always loved words, so I used writing as a means of expressing what I dared not say aloud. I would journal some, but mostly I found poetry to be a favored means of expression. It also had the added benefit of ambiguity, should someone read it uninvited.

I still write poetry sometimes.

I find that writing gives more clarity to what is really going on with me. It is also a safe way to release pent up emotions, frustration, or anger. In my youth these were things that were not safe to express. Later, these were things I did not want to pollute the lives of others with.

Art is another lifelong friend of mine. I create art to express what there are no words for, the feelings that are too scrambled for logical and clear communication. A viewer may interpret what I generate in unintended ways, but the freshness of new perspectives can reveal things to me that I did not know I meant, but should have.

Both art and writing are pure medicines for the soul, with no dangerous side effects on the labels. Music, especially, seems to be a universal curative.

Try to do any or all. It doesn't matter if you are good at it. Do it to express you, as a means of getting those feelings out and into fresh air. Some of it will be good. Some of it won't be. But this isn't school. You aren't graded on the quality or rote memorization. This isn't about pleasing others. It is about having a safe place to go with what is within you, when what you have is too personal to share, or when there is no one you can safely share it with.

This is a way to be your own support. If you come from an abusive background, it is all the more important to learn.

If you choose an expression through writing, it might be equally important to keep your journals in a safe place, where only you can have access to them. What is in them is no one's business but your own. Sharing is your choice to make, not an obligation to anyone else.

You have to face your anger, pain, problems, and issues to recover. Don't sabotage your process or set yourself up for failure by trying to do it all at once. Tackle it a little at a time.

The one thing you must not do is pass your problems on to someone else. That doesn't help you heal. It only compounds the issue for you, and adds to the woes of someone who may be dealing with her own problems.

By not dealing with the effects of trauma and abuse you internalize it further, making you even more physically, mentally, and emotionally unhealthy. Furthermore, you add to the risk of passing these poisons on to those around you, especially your children. You have heard this called the *cycle of abuse*.

My father's father was abusive. My father chose this path for himself. We all choose it, or not, at some point in our lives. Because my brother did not have understanding or an outlet for the pain he suffered at the hands of our father, he because abusive. *He chose to be*. It's a pattern as simple to see as counting one-two-three. Even if you are the victim of deliberate abuse, at some point you have to decide who you will be.

Another way we cope with this cycle is through self-harm. I was suicidal. My sister became an alcoholic. For others it might manifest itself through drugs, prostitution, cutting, or any number of destructive behaviors. The common root is self-loathing. If your parents attached no value to you, it is hard to value yourself. And if you lack that basic self-esteem you will attract the predators who have no value for you, either, because they feel it in your energy.

To combat this, you must learn that there is an inherent value to every human being, whether you see it or not. And, especially, you must see this in yourself.

I wish I had known this. I wish I had had someone to tell me all of this, like I'm telling it to you. It might have saved many people a lot of hurt.

When the hellish reign of my father was over, I was wild with pain. This soon turned to anger. I shared it quite liberally through my teens and early twenties. I did not have to do this. *I chose to.*

Then one day I said something flippant and cruel to someone I loved. I saw the pain in his eyes, as if I had truly done him physical harm. I was astonished and felt awful, but the damage was done. I had no idea how hurtful I had become, or how entitled to it I had become. I saw myself as having become no better than the people who had visited so much hurt upon me.

It was a huge awakening. It changed me.

Afterwards I was far more careful about how I expressed myself, but I was still very reactionary. I would become angry at every perceived slight or injustice.

It was exhausting.

Eventually I realized that I was controlled by every event and person that displeased me. For years my moods had risen and plummeted like a roller coaster. By the time I understood this I was weary of the ride.

I decided to quit reacting and to begin choosing an action. I learned to let the little things go, and to study the larger issues. I couldn't change the people who affected me, and shouldn't spend my energy trying to. What I could do is change who or what I was to them. Likewise, I couldn't change events, but I could change how I responded.

Learning and implementing this gave me a powerful addition to my pallet of healing. This is a must for you, too. Become action-oriented rather than reactionary. You will find amazing power in it.

This will help you to not take your anger and pain out on others. Everyone suffers in life. You did not invent suffering. It is not unique to you. Everyone experiences it at some point.

There is a matter of degree, of course. Not everyone is raped or beaten or abused. Or raped *and* beaten *and* abused. Or/and abandoned. There might not be anyone around you who has endured any of these things, or be able to imagine or understand your individual past.

But this does not mean that they do not have their own pasts, their own secret terrors and fears; their own pain and suffering. They don't need you to add to their burdens by taking your issues out on them, any more than you need theirs. Just be aware that even suppressed anger comes out in passive aggressive or self-destructive ways. Don't punish yourself, and don't punish those around you. Don't be the thing that put you in this position.

If you have been abused, your abuser is not who you need to model yourself after. They did not know how to handle their anger, pain, and other issues. This is the cycle you have to break.

When a situation angers me, I take a step back from it, engaging my Observing Self. Very often, I will say little or nothing at the moment. I become that observer, taking it all in, in an attempt to understand what has happened. I try to think the moment all the way through. Then I choose how to respond. If it is something that I can't do anything about, or if it's actually not really important, I let it go.

This is not to invalidate my original response, though. The bigger the problem, the more time I may take to sort it out (action, not reaction). If what angered me needs to be addressed, I choose my timing and words with care. I state the facts as I see them, how I feel about them, and what I choose to do about it.

The operative word here is "choose," not "react." For instance, I *choose* to use physical exercise as a healthy means of releasing tension and anger. In general application, this beats even art and writing as means to release. It helps bring the body into closer balance with the mind and the spirit.

But whatever means you choose, you have to learn to either use your pain and anger, or let it go, in order to move forward. If you keep it, then you stay in the same place. Take control of it. Do not let it control you any longer.

And never forget that we are all energy. But there are different kinds of energy, and not all combine in compatible mixtures. When mixed together, some are (to further the analogy) explosive.

I have had a number of personal relationships where we brought out the worst in each other. This repeated experience led me to adopt the rule that, when I can no longer be kind, I can no longer be in the relationship. I do not like to hurt people for any reason. But I also do not like being hurt. As I have a strong survival instinct, this can lead me to be especially hurtful in retaliation.

This is not a healthy way to be. So I direct the energy I would waste in spite and retribution to avoidance or Flight. I am in the position in my life where I can decide whether or not someone is good or bad for me; if he or she brings out my worst, or comes dangerously close to abusing me in any manner.

Pain in life is inescapable. Abuse is not. Avoid abusive relationships, and you have done half the work of avoiding becoming an abuser yourself.

You are responsible for how you manage your feelings. If you are an abuse victim, you have probably learned plenty about how not to handle anger. The problem may be that no one ever taught you the correct way to handle it, or demonstrated mature, civilized examples.

Anger is not a bad emotion, in itself. We have developed it for the same reason we walk upright; it works for us. It can tell us much about the situation we are in. If you perceive that you are being misused or taken advantage of, it is natural to be angry. But if anger is your automatic response to every event, then you must explore what is in you that reacts that way, because not everything in the world is targeted at you.

So you are still the one responsible. It is imperative for you to learn to control it, limit it, or work it out through whatever expression works best for you. The more you do this, the more it becomes a natural response, because you have built the pathways for it.

Of course, other emotions may be just as overwhelming or debilitating. It depends on the individual and the circumstances. Grief, sadness, regret; any of these can demand more from us beyond what they actually deserve. When they present themselves, I spend time with them, but I don't let them dominate my life. I give them what is required, but no more. Then I move on. Even when I am grieving from time to time (perhaps the touchiest "negative" emotion for me to deal with), I might do so with a smile, just because I knew the person I am missing at all.

The point is, be with it, whatever it is. But do not get lost in it. You've a life to live.

Child Abuse and the Tribe

To abuse a child is to cripple them before they can walk. It disorganizes their brain, leaving gaps in a period of development that is critical to survival.

If there is something more cruel in this world, I do not know what it is.

Children learn by example. If they are busy trying to survive they aren't learning to live. They sacrifice education and normal social interaction. They learn abuse and cruelty.

We are genetically designed for tribal living, where the community's children are everyone's children. And yet modern life leaves us isolated and scattered. Community is as necessary as food and shelter. It ensures survival of both the individual and the group. Community is working together and supporting one another.

Trauma and abuse can be devastating handicaps in a child's life. This isn't to say that they cannot turn out well, but it is likely that they will never quite be what they could have been. A parent's job is to protect, nurture, and educate. Children are defenseless little beings in a dangerous world.

My experience has shown me that filling in some of the gaps is easier once the child develops reasoning skills. As young teens they can begin to make sense of it and begin to make some of their own choices.

The treatment center I work at follows a model researched and designed by Dr. Bruce Perry, from the ChildTrauma Academy, based in Houston, Texas. He works with early childhood development using modalities derived from the Neurosequential Model of Therapeutics. Dr. Perry advocates art, music, movement, and massage as valid methods of treatment for traumatized, abused, and neglected children.

This confirms what my research and experimentation had shown to be a valid understanding of the biological and psychological impact of trauma, and a path to healing, for both children and adults. More importantly, where I had to rely upon personal experience and ambiguous data to formulate my theories and practices, Dr. Perry and his staff have the resources for methodical laboratory experimentation. They have even developed a method of diagnosis by which they can chart the developmental gaps.

Of course, even without trauma or abuse to blame, adolescent choices are not always going to be wise ones. Research published as I write confirms what any parent of a teenager can tell us. The human brain does not fully develop until we are in our mid-twenties. In brief, we don't need outside trauma to do damage to ourselves.

But with trauma and abuse to complicate our perception of the world, we have almost no other choice than to make matters worse. It increases the likelihood of re-creation as a means to make sense of what was done to us.

Even children do this. And if their pain is intense and incomprehensible, they can become little time bombs.

This is the child that I was, and the children that I work with. In their need to diffuse the "bomb" (bleed off the pressure), they are prone to self-harm or aggression on others. This is often the point where the world becomes the parent in the form of either the streets or the state. If the child is very, very lucky, there will be strong, healthy adults to guide them back and to help mend the damage.

This is not easy to do. Not only does it seem that there is more damage than there are healers to help, but all too often the children that need it are difficult to manage. Too many "solutions" only aggravate the condition. Too many drugs are dispensed that create completely new problems.

So these children grow up - that is, age - trying to sort out their problems with inadequate support, and often find new kinds of trouble; too often self-destructive to some degree. But with any luck they mature with time, developing safer coping mechanisms and more adult understanding of the unfair events that caused them so much trouble and pain. With luck they become decent people with decent lives, in spite of their histories.

With luck.

Sadly, there seems to be little enough luck to go around these days. These "lucky" ones are the minority. For too many of the rest there are the "lives of quiet desperation" (Thoreau), the streets, or even prisons. And there is always death.

They are victims as wronged as anyone else subjected to a crime, but the crime visited upon them is too easily made invisible. Modern culture is more comfortable with, at best, withholding comfort and consideration; ignoring them. At its worst, society is derisive and blames these victims for their predicaments.

The breakdown of the community and our failure to properly care for the vulnerable in our society is becoming ever more prominent and damning. Our collective propensity to blame the victim (even when we say we don't) and the victim's tendency to be victims (even when they say it's not their fault) puts us in conflicting situations.

But all of this was the Big Picture. Let's bring this back home.

To you.

If you are reading this because you are dealing with the effects of having been victimized, then you are taking a good step forward. But don't forget; no matter what has happened to you, it is your responsibility to work hard on your recovery. This book is not a magic wand in your hands. The magic wands *are* your hands, real and metaphorical. My purpose is to help you find them and use them.

And if you are reading this because someone you know needs help, or you simply need to "save the world," period, good for you. But that isn't going to stop me from telling you the obvious; it is our responsibility as a community to help both those who are trying to help themselves, and those who do not know how.

Getting Free

There is no one-size-fits-all cure for victims of abuse and trauma to heal themselves with, and I am not going to deceive you by pretending there is.

I can offer a selection of suggestions, though. Consider them to be starting points, places you can use and be inspired to find your own ideas by. Of course, if you work through a couple and have a sudden healing breakthrough, then you are welcome to tell everyone you know what a genius I am.

Let go of the relationships that are too unhealthy to ever recover, no matter with whom they are. But salvage the ones you can by changing them. Not everyone you know will be resistant to the alterations you feel you need to make to heal. These will be good people to keep at whatever level you feel comfortable with.

Let go of the idea that you deserve the miserable life you have, that the things that happened to you, you had coming. You may not consciously believe this, but you have to look at it just the same. If there is any possibility that your subconscious harbors this attitude, you have no choice but to dig it out and deal with it.

As discussed earlier, this will likely be the most difficult aspect of your healing path. It is hard work. It may be deeply imprinted in your brain and your subconscious because the abuse started early in life. But healing demands that you search for it, no matter how difficult the task is. Just knowing that it is there gives you a powerful tool to exorcise it with.

But don't obsess about rooting it all out. Likely you will always carry some degree of this self-castigation with you, like the seed of a weed. Your affirmations are excellent garden hoes for this. Refuse to believe that you are nothing and that you deserved such treatment. The seed might not completely die, but the weed won't grow.

In as detached a manner as you can manage, look at every relationship in your life (Observing Self). Observe your interactions, both verbal and nonverbal (body language to physical threats). Who are *you* in the interaction? Who are *they*? Is it healthy or harmful to you? If it is unhealthy, how long has it been that way? How deep are the patterns of behavior? And, finally, could you change it?

If you need something to compare yours to, observe the healthy relationships of others.

Because humans are what we are, our first temptation is to try to change those around us before we recognize that it is ourselves that need the change. I spent a lot of energy trying to do just that before I figured out that I couldn't change someone who did not want (or agree that there was a need) to change.

(Predators, especially, will not willingly alter their behavior. If they would, then they wouldn't be predators.)

But if you are in a harmful relationship, and you reasonably suspect that the issues are not just yours, do not waste time and energy that can be better used in other elements of healing. You cannot have healthy relationships with unhealthy people. "Downsize" the nature of the relationship, or let it go.

Over the years I let go of my parents, my brother, my sister, and a number of "friends" I acquired during more reckless, less discriminating, and even self-destructive periods of my life. This was no easier for me than it will be for you. There was a sizable cost. It left a deep sort of loneliness that no one else can fill, especially the Mommy and Daddy roles.

I chose loneliness over abuse and baggage that would kill me to carry any further.

The passing of time has brought its changes. I have a loving family, both of my own making and the one that welcomed me into it as daughter and sister, and some wonderful, caring friends. My life is happy and full. I may still miss what those other people could have and should have been to me, out of sweetly sad sentiment. I even still love them. I love everyone I ever loved. Trying to destroy that in me only hurt me worse.

But I wanted peace for myself. I wanted to not have to fight and protect myself, especially from those whose job it was to protect me. I wanted to not be held back from making a life for myself, and discouraged from even trying, by the very people who should have been behind me all the way.

It was them or me, and I realized that I was under no obligation to suffer so someone else could exercise their brutality.

The challenges that those of us who were abused as children face are daunting. It is not just one or two events that we have to recover from, as trauma can be when deliberate abuse is not involved. If something like physical injury is involved, our trauma may be visible to the whole world, and the world may feel sorry for us and make accommodations.

This is not to say there is no internal and lasting damage, the "invisible" kind that abuse imparts. But by its nature, abuse tends to be invisible to the world. Abusers, like predators, like to do their dirty work away from the eyes of the world. And unlike the trauma caused by surgery or and accident, they like to do it over and over and over again.

That trauma becomes deeply ingrained in us, the victims. But the expectations of our culture and society are that we get over our wounds (visible eventually; invisible doesn't even count), hide them, and go on to be model taxpayers and consumers. These wounds make us too collectively uncomfortable to even discuss.

The existence of this book demonstrates my position on the subject. I am anti-hide-it and pro-recovery. And we all have the same obligations to be the best people we can be, and to help our fellow humans to do the same, even if it means flying in the face of cultural denial. Denial doesn't heal anything. People with abuse issues they haven't dealt with are often reactionary and destructive. Some become dangers to themselves and others. Like it or not, societal norms or not, this means their problems are our problems.

We have to face this black plague that many experts believe to be a viable threat to the stability and growth of all societies. If the harm caused by abuse and trauma is not compassionately and generously dealt with, it will continue to erode our culture until the minority of victims becomes the majority of everyone affected by it, and we - you and me - become the actual burdens on society that society says we are.

This idea seriously offends me, because I believe that given the tools to recover, and given the understanding of what truly happened to them, people will work their butts off to make their lives right and healthy again. The naysayers - those who are biased against and judgmental of anyone whose life experience and worldview doesn't mirror their own - are wrong.

The people I know who have recovered from such histories are amazing individuals. By "recovering" I mean managing the impact it had on their lives. Every day they work to heal a little more. They are mindful of their issues, and manage them so they have a minimum impact on anyone else.

They accomplished this with a little help. Now they give it.

Brain function is connected to early brain development. Because of my history of abuse and the effects of PTSD, I easily experience primal fear. It is the first place I go when I feel threatened. I then become survival-oriented.

This is a deep internal process and reaction to a threat long since passed. I am mindful of this but, even after all these years - even knowing everything about abuse and PTSD that I do - it is difficult to control. But I must, because the alternative is for it to control me. Sitting quietly and doing the hu gong breath helps. I breathe in calm and breathe out fear. Self-regulation is a difficult thing to have to do when your body has lost the ability to do it on its own. It takes conscious work, vigilance, and patience on your part and sometimes the part of others. It takes *intention*.

There are remnants of my old life in my cells and the wiring of my brain. As I mentioned above, I can still revert to behavior triggered by events perceived to be similar to the original abuse that brought me to this condition in the first place. I am better and healthier than I have ever been before, but my recovery continues. As I did in the beginning, I may still need to expel fear, grief, self-loathing, and many other negative feelings from my energy through yoga or breathing or meditation. I worked hard to change how I think about some things, and still do. This is work with a sizable payoff.

I don't mind that my brain is wired differently. It makes it easy for me to "think outside the box." As a result of my experiences, I have more sympathy for the human and animal plight than I might otherwise have had. It runs deep in me. I know the depths of suffering first hand. I feel it in others, and see it around me.

Because I have "redirected" my experience, I try to do something about what I see. Some of the pain and trauma can be loved away. To love and be loved, with no conditions. Whether it is a pet or a friend or even a stranger, the balm of love heals much.

It is good to know the truth about yourself, outside of what others have told you. We all have things wonderful and terrible within us. I polish my goodness and stay mindful of my shadow. I know each side intimately, and I don't let others color my perception of them. I am always honest with myself, and know when to seek out wise counsel to keep myself in check.

No one deserves abuse.

The Instinctual Self

Our bodies are amazingly instinctual. They become even more so as a result of trauma.

Instincts are the felt sense I described earlier; reactions triggered by unperceived stimuli. When my muscles tense, my breathing gets shallow, and I'm hyperalert, I am sensing the possibility of danger. I trust my instincts when it comes to certain people and situations.

I am sensitive to the types of energy that child molesters, abusers, and just plain bad and mean people radiate. I avoid even eye contact with people who don't "feel" right, so that they don't have a chance to read something in me that they can hook onto. In my minds' eye I make them invisible to me, and me to them. I draw in my energy. If you can learn to do these techniques, you will find that they work well for camouflaging yourself from the types of predators you habitually attract.

I avoid interacting with anyone my instinctual self says no to. I can be polite in social situations, but I keep myself unavailable to their needs.

There are times when this part of me is hyperactive or reactive. I still give my body/mind what it asks for; protection.

Be on your own side. Listen to your instincts. Better to do that and be wrong than to ignore the signals and be sorry.

This is not the same thing as being fearful. Learn what your fears are and be mindful of them in your life. When fear arises, observe your situation and ask yourself if it is justified. Or is the situation only new and outside your comfort zone? It is not a good reason if it is about avoiding life and new growth and experiences. You have to coax yourself from your shell and cautiously test the waters. Test, not avoid.

Remember Fight, Flight, or Freeze. We have our "favorite"

responses that come from our experiences of what has and hasn't worked for us in the past. My primary responses are Fight, then Freeze.

The Fight response can be very destructive. You know that with a history of trauma or abuse you are overly sensitive. Under the right circumstances, even triggers I thought I had banished can recur and put me on the defensive. When that happens I try to redirect my energy into something useful, or even deliberately choose the Flight response, and go for a walk.

What it tells me about myself or the situation I am in is important. I may need to redefine my boundaries - detach - with a person or a situation. In the past this has meant that I need to find a new job, alter a relationship, or change something within myself.

Even now it can still as easily be a problem within me as it is with someone or something outside myself. I assess the situation as honestly as possible, own my part in it, and decide what to do about it. Still, sometimes I just can't figure the problem out. Rather than force it, I let it ride and play itself out, limiting the energy I give to it so that I don't shortchange other easier or more important tasks.

The Freeze response is what keeps us locked in a behavior or pattern, or stuck in a situation. It can be in parallel with or connected to learned helplessness. This response is physically the hardest on your body. There is no discharge of pent up energy as there is in Fight and Flight. The energy just gets stuck in your body, trashing your nervous system and ultimately the rest of your body, including your bones, organs, and skin.

You have to learn to release this energy in positive ways. Activities such as mentioned earlier can help calm your nervous system, release the stifled energy, and serve to "defrost" you. Exercise, yoga, breathing, art, writing, music, or anything that gives you release are essential to your healing process.

Even though it is not at the top of my personal list, Flight is a better choice than my natural inclinations give it credit for. It is certainly far better than Freeze if, for no other reason, it gives your body and psyche the opportunity to discharge the energy generated by threat.

Of course, this isn't necessarily an extreme run-for-your-life situation. Verbal abuse, or even an intimidating presence should be able to trigger Flight. So, too, can tension or frustration. Depending upon your history and tolerance, these can be as dangerous as violence. When I find myself faced with these, even if only slightly, I might make myself choose the Flight response, even if it is only by going for a walk. Or, in some cases, I might develop an "exit strategy." Because I have control of my life, and am no longer in threatening environments of any kind, this doesn't have to be big and elaborate. I don't even have to believe that I will act on it. It can be enough just to know that I have a way out and that I am not trapped.

The point is, I am making a choice. Additionally, I am exercising a response that I did not use enough when I was younger. Also, I am giving my body what it wants. If I cooperate with it, it is much kinder to me.

If you think that one of the responses is missing from your menu, work with it to get it functioning properly. We have all three of these for good reasons. Without them, the human species would have died out millennia ago.

So if your Fight response isn't all it should be, take a self-defense class or boxing or anything that involves a controlled threat. Or if your Freeze response doesn't stop your mouth from needing the Fight response, you need to consciously practice with it. Before you fight, pause and think your actions or words through first. And if you habitually Freeze before you flee, you need to practice walking away and letting go.

Pay attention to your instinctual self and be in control of it to the best of your ability. Self-mastery isn't easy for anyone.

It's just harder for some. Consciously build the pathways that support it.

That is what I have done to bring my life and my world together in harmony. I do not fight unless absolutely necessary. I do not walk away unless it is absolutely the best solution. And I take the actions that eliminate stress and "frost" from my body and my energy.

Boundaries, and a Few Exercises

If you are an American, your common boundary - "personal space" - is about two feet in most directions. People considered to be friends can move in and out of this zone without notice, but if strangers or enemies enter it we might become uncomfortable; our space is "invaded."

(There are cultural and environmental differences in this measure. Americans from densely populated cities will, by necessity, have a more contracted personal zone. So, too, might individuals from other countries.)

However, many of my clients who have a history of abuse have severely contracted boundaries. This can be a foot or less. And I have worked with individuals whose auras have been completely destroyed by their experiences. They have no sense of containment or any sense of the boundaries of others.

Mental and emotional boundaries are equally complicated. As a general rule I go by what does or doesn't feel right to me, trusting my felt sense and observing the responses of others to me. Just remember that this is the easy part. It comes after learning to differentiate between threatening and non-threatening situations, prioritize these, and self-regulate responses.

Spiritual boundaries are our moral codes. There are long-standing arguments regarding their source; culture and environment versus instinct. For the most part, I come down on the side of instinct, as in we "instinctively know the difference between right and wrong." This isn't to say that culture and societal norms don't have their contributions, but I believe that spirituality - the thing outside of us that we know is there and is bigger than we are - provides us with our great moral compass.

But in some instances, these boundaries are the ones most

easily and thoughtlessly violated. Perhaps this is because it is a boundary even more "invisible" than personal space. Believers and non-believers of all persuasions - Christian, Jew, Moslems, atheists - cross this border every time they deny the right of every human being to know god as they wish. . . or not.

These boundaries are your birthright. It is up to you to claim them, own them, and define them for yourself. Your obligation here might include providing guidance for others, but never enforcement. Everyone has the same right as you.

Pay attention and learn to know where you feel powerless, helpless, or violated, and learn to exert your boundaries. Expand your personal space and your aura until you are comfortable in your world and feel protected in healthy ways. If this is new to you, it will take courage and strength. But the attempt will create a feedback loop for you. The more you try, the stronger and more courageous you will become, and so the more you can do. This is taking care of you.

The Aura Shield for a Sense of Containment

If you are really sensitive to the energy of other people, have poor boundaries, or lack a strong sense of yourself, try this exercise.

Close your eyes. Imagine a bubble that completely surrounds you. Now imagine your very best self coming through the top of your head in the form of light. Let it fill the bubble.

I do this if I am feeling depleted or vulnerable. It is a comforting exercise.

Warriors and Mirrors

This is an exercise I do if I am feeling unpleasant energy being directed towards me and I feel unprotected. I imagine two warriors in my aura. One is at my solar plexus, and the other has my back. They protect my energy. We will look at these locations when I cover chakras.

If someone really doesn't like me and it disturbs my calm, I make sure that I am not sending out any energy of my own. Then, in my imagination, I surround them with mirrors to reflect their energy back. This gives them the opportunity to understand that the problem is their issue, not mine.

And if I am not in a great place and fear that someone will detect it, and it doesn't feel safe to me, I surround myself with mirrors to contain my energy and aura so the person I am concerned about can't get a reading on me.

These exercises work well for me, and also for the clients I recommend them to.

Transference and Countertransference

This is a very troublesome issue when it arises in relationships. It is when people mirror ourselves back to us, or we do that to them. It is often initiated by some kind of trigger, theirs or ours, and is not entirely conscious. It can be difficult to recognize when it is occurring and, if we don't figure it out, it can be a little crazy-making.

When I first started working with children I had a client I'll call Ted. Ted had a history of abuse, including sexual abuse. Something I did triggered him (I never identified what). He then projected onto me the role of abuser.

As I have my own abuse issues, this is a role I do not wish to be put into. The occurrence, in turn, triggered me to a degree. I not only felt that I had harmed him, but my own feelings of guilt and shame resurfaced.

Fortunately his therapist was present, and explained to me - with the event as example - about *transference* and *countertransference*.   Transference is a psychological phenomenon whereby the feelings caused in one person by another are unconsciously redirected to an unrelated third. Countertransference is redirection of a therapist's feelings or emotions towards a client.

Upon my own review of the session, I came to realize that I had been staying well inside my own safe boundaries about abuse and healthy touch. My countertransference of this is what made me feel that I had harmed Ted.

Ted dropped out of the program afterwards, wanting nothing more to do with me. In his mind, I was like - and perhaps the same - person who had abused him. As it is the policy of my program that the child-client is in complete control, I gave him all the space from me he wanted.

For three months we largely ignored each other, although sometimes I would greet him in the halls, or smile when I saw him. I just let him be.

Then one day when I went to pick up another child from his class, Ted opened the door for me. Rather playfully, he said, "Please don't beat me," and smiled.

I was shocked, but quickly assured him that I never would. I then asked him why he would say such a thing to me. "I don't know," he said with a shrug, and sat down.

Not long after, he asked to come back to the program. The work we did together for the next year was remarkably successful. By the time he left the school he had become a far different child from the one I had originally known. He was more relaxed and playful.

This is what happens with transference-countertransference. Had the therapist not been present I may well have believed that I had somehow caused the harm I was there to heal, and quit my job. But I got to learn how powerful T-CT can be. I triggered him; he triggered me. Like a veteran soldier in a minefield, I know what to look for now.

Another example of T-CT is when I have a client who feels like they are the lowest of the low. I have noticed that, in some cases, others behave towards them as if this is true. Even I have, without thinking, reacted to certain individuals in this way. In either instance, I stop and, if nothing else, ask myself if this person is truly the unworthy creature that they are assumed to be, and deserving of my opinion or treatment of them.

They rarely are.

Through whatever social, cultural, or spiritual mechanism is at work here, we pick up on this weakness and react to them as predators do to prey. Sadly, this tells me that even the best intentioned of us can have the worst we can be lurking inside. By letting their self-perception guide our perception of them, we can actually come nearer to being what they think they are than they do.

Just as bad, our response can only reinforce this negative self-image, making it a self-fulfilling prophecy. Adults who believe the worst of themselves can become that very thing.

The deeper this pathway, the harder it is to change. Hard, but not impossible. The kinder and more understanding you are to someone like this, the more humane you treat them, the more you see yourself in them, then the more it undermines that negative self-image. And the more deliberately kind you are, the more naturally kind you become. The people around you will feel this, and some may even begin to blossom.

You consciously decide who you will be.

This has all been a warning. While you are working on your issues, it is common for transference to occur. All it takes is strong emotion and a trigger or two (yours or someone else's). You can set yourself back.

That is why it is best to just walk away when issues arise or conflict. Give it space to defuse, and see if it will sort itself out on its own. As was the case with Ted, my own projections have the potential to create a new mess. By walking away when I did, it gave us both the space we needed to sort things out.

So be careful of what you project as an image, and what presentation you let other people project to you. Test what you think you see against what you know. Measure the truth of it, and be mindful of it. This set of circumstances can be brutal on relationships if you aren't.

Your Body and Health: "Self-Medication" (Massage) and Posture

India and China have the oldest health systems in the world, commonly called *Chinese medicine* and *ayurvedic medicine* (which means "the complete knowledge for long life"). What makes these systems different from traditional Western medicine is that they consider the person as a whole, an organism whose different parts are connected and interrelated, and which affect the health and function of each other.

The basis of the Chinese system is the belief that we have lines of energy called *meridians* that govern and connect each organ to all others. Also, each organ has a *pulse* that can be detected and measured at points on the wrists. In Chinese medicine, this tells the doctor more than your heart is beating.

Each organ also has an emotion that it is intimately connected to. For instance, anger comes from and affects the liver, grief does the same with the lungs, and kidneys are the life force. Blockages in any organ impact the organs above and below it. One might have excessive energy, while the other may be deficient.

A doctor of Chinese medicine can tell by the quality of a pulse the health of each organ. He might treat imbalances with herbal decoctions, or acupressure or acupuncture to bring meridians back into alignment.

I can personally attest that this is a balanced, natural, and effective treatment of bodily ailments.

In ayurvedic medical theory practitioners analyze your body type according to three categories, and assign treatments according to the needs and imbalances detected. These body types are called *doshas*, and most of us are combinations of two or all three.

One dosha is called *vāta*, which is the leanest body type. Vātas are full of energy, so they are advised to avoid ingesting stimulants of any kind. Sugar and caffeine feed what they may already have too much of; energy.

Pitta is another body type. Physically, pitas are of medium build, but their nature tends to be fiery. Spicy foods can aggravate this quality, and so should be avoided.

Kapha is the largest of the body types. They have slower than normal metabolisms, and if they get out of balance they can stop metabolizing foods correctly. This makes it extremely difficult for them to lose weight.

Herbs, diet, and sometimes bodywork can help keep the doshas in balance. When the body is in balance, health is the result.

It is amusingly human that most people are attracted to what they shouldn't do. For instance I, as a combination vāta and pitta, like caffeine and hot and spicy foods. A kapha will prefer heavy comfort foods. We may enjoy doing this, but we pay for it in physical and emotional health. Like any important machine, the body needs proper care to function well. If this is given, your body feels better, and so does the inner you.

So healthy food is a must. The more processed a food is, the less nutritional value it has, and the more the body needs to feel satisfied. Fats and salt and sugars cause our appetite regulators to short out, so we don't stop when we should. We take in empty calories to make up for shortages in quality and nutrition. The body wants whole grains, fresh fruits and vegetables, nuts, and beans. The meats it asks for should be seldom, and lean. It can go a lot further on a little of these than it can on whole bags of chips and cartons of ice cream.

Not only can proper changes in diet improve the body, they can also be medicinal. When we have a history of abuse or trauma, our body can take on the role of enemy. Because it is the vehicle of the pain we have endured we may acquire self-destructive habits, or disassociate from it. Obviously neither is a healthy approach to healing. Our bodies are the homes of our souls, and what we do to them, we do to our spirits. If, in spite of everything that has happened to damage us, we choose to take the best possible care of our physical self with a nutritional diet, we will have a greater opportunity for healthy, healing, happy lives as whole, integrated beings.

It is important to remember this. Because our Western cultures teach us to think in fragmented terms about our bodies (the hip bone is not connected to the knee bone), we have to make the effort to consider the whole person. We are body, mind, and spirit, sloppily wrapped in a package of ourselves.

So, to emphasize: If you have a diet heavy in junk food your organs and body will suffer, and you simply won't feel good, even if you aren't doing yourself immediate damage. I follow an 80/20 rule in my diet. Healthy foods composed of fresh ingredients and prepared at home make up 80% of my diet. The remaining 20% is my wiggle room where, if I have or simply want to, I can grab something on the go, or have that sweet dessert.

(Just a note; the more time I have spent following a fresh diet, the less attracted I am to the fast and junky foods that are so available on grocery shelves and chain restaurants. They simply taste bad.)

The healthier I eat the better I feel, and so the better my mind functions. What can be simpler than that? You may want to beg off by saying that you are too busy to put that much time and effort into cooking, but you will be doing yourself a disservice. I am a busy woman, far more than I ever imagined I would grow up to be. So one of my tricks is to cook ahead and refrigerate or freeze ingredients or even whole meals. This way I have the healthy foods that I need available at a moment's notice.

Of course, diet is only one part of a healthy life. That's why they usually put "and exercise" in the ads for magic weight-loss pills. Aside from that, there is a simple fact: Your body was designed to be used. It was built to work hard, walk long distances, and breathe deeply.

You use it or lose it. Losing it only adds to our problems. Action helps solve them. The absolute best way to deal with stress of almost any kind is to do physical exercise. But it is important for you to know that, if you have abuse or trauma in your history, it is very common to resist this type of self-care.

Too much exercise can be a stressor of its own. For some of us, as example, even the elevated breathing in aerobic exercise can be a trigger for our issues, linking to either our own breathing during an event, or the breathing of someone else during something that should not have happened. (It connects to the fear we may have experienced.)

My personal preference is plain old hatha yoga. It is relaxation exercise that helps to unify the body, mind, and spirit. Tai chi and chi gong have the same effect.

When I do yoga I relax into the pose for as much as several minutes. I breathe out the stuck energy, and just feel my body. I listen to what it has to say.

Listen to what your body feels like it wants when you are working with it. It can't lie to you. Find a way to give it what it asks for.

Walking is another favorite. In some systems walking is a meditation technique. What they all have in common is the release of stress. Releasing stress in the body is key to self-regulation.

I manage my body with as simple and as natural ways as I can. My garden gives me some of my food. As far as possible, I manage health issues with herbs. And I exercise with yoga, walking, and gardening.

I also get regular massage. Touch is a very real biological need. Babies deprived of it have been known to die. Having grown up in a threatening environment, I learned early to armor myself by tightening my muscles. This means that I hold a lot of tension in my body. Unattended, this makes me a stress ball. So, when I am tense but I don't have access to my regular body workers, I do what I call Poor Man's Massage.

Poor Man's Massage

Tennis balls can be very good friends for what they can do for your back. On each side of your spine are a group of muscles called the erector spinae. These are the muscles that keep you sitting and standing upright. If you suffer back pain, they are likely the source of it. Fortunately, you don't have to have a sixty-dollar-an-hour body worker to find relief. This is where the tennis balls come in.

Lay on a rug. Place a tennis ball on each side of your spine, high in your shoulders, or just on one side (never directly on the backbone). Bend your knees, then using your legs to push your body, slowly roll the length of your spine. If needed, you can increase the pressure by lifting your pelvis off the floor. When you find a particularly painful spot, stop rolling and just hang out there. Breathe through the discomfort to release the tension. I often use a single ball so I can focus on each specific problem. If, for instance, it is in my low back, I position the tennis ball between my 12th rib and the hipbone. Leaning into it can hurt, but it solves the problem.

You can work your glutes the same way. Position the ball on either side of your tail bone and work around the femur in the hip socket. Stay off the bones themselves, as it is not comfortable or necessary to be on them.

If tennis balls aren't quite hard enough, and you are tough enough, softballs or baseballs can serve. For some of my specific issues I even use golf balls to pinpoint trigger points. (Trigger points will be the most painful spots in the muscle.)

Another approach for the back is to use a narrow pillow positioned in the upper back, because most of us slouch, and the mid-back is stressed as a result. Lie back on the pillow until you feel relief.

Like the back, the neck is a source of major complaints for many. After all, its main job is to hold up an object the size and weight of a bowling ball. You don't want to use the tennis or other balls for your neck, though. Instead, roll up a towel. Lying down, place it in the curve of your neck. Look straight ahead (up). Relax.

Spend a few minutes looking up, then turn your head to one side. Relax there, too, then turn to the other side for a few minutes. To get the most help out of this you have to relax into each position, letting your neck self-correct.

I do the back pillow and neck roll at the same time, along with the hu gong breathing technique to release stuck energy. Twenty minutes of this and I am brand new. If you will commit to trying it once, you will find a way to add it to your day.

Your body is the expert about itself. It will tell you what it wants or needs. Use pillows or different sizes and shapes to prop it in the positions it feels like it wants, then relax and rest that way.

Help give your body what it wants by using these props. Relaxation begins with your attitude. Don't lay there thinking about all the other stuff you should be doing. This is just as important as anything else. The meditation I have encouraged you to practice is to help you relax your mind, and that will help you with your body.

And don't neglect or forget about posture. I wouldn't bring it up if it wasn't a huge issue for most of us. Odds are, your posture is lousy. It's probably that way because you don't pay attention to it. But it affects how you feel. Your mother was right, at least in this case. Sit up straight by scooting your butt all the way back in a chair, then lean back and hold your head upright. You don't need to be that close to a computer screen, anyway. You don't need to slouch to watch television. It is easier to breathe now, and that in itself changes your mood.

The same thing happens when your correct how you stand.

It doesn't have to be at attention. Just stand straight, knees slightly bent, pelvis tucked in and head up. It might take some awareness in the beginning. Correcting bad habits always does. But you need to replace an old habit with a new one.

Besides, this helps make you look proud and confident. If you have this on the outside, it will make its way into your inside. This is just another way of rewriting your history.

Your body might not like it because it is stuck in the old ways, but you can teach it, and have yet another excuse to lay down for a few minutes. Lay on a small, firm pillow placed mid-back, so that it pushes your chest forward. This may be uncomfortable in the beginning, but it is because you are retraining the muscles of their real jobs.

Re-Educating

Much of what we have discussed to this point can be grouped under the heading, *Re-Education*. There's been talk about re-educating your brain to process thoughts differently, and re-educating those thoughts, themselves. These last few pages have been about re-educating your body, in part so that your brain does not perceive your body as the enemy. Your body is your friend. There's not much you can do without it. Abuse and trauma are the enemy, and there's nothing you can't do when you conquer them. Help you body get what it wants. Learn to relax it, be kind to it, and reclaim it as your own.

The body perceives hunger, thirst, and lack of sleep as stressors. Stress is just as damaging to it as PTSD. So eat correctly, stay hydrated, exercise, and rest.

Sleep

In our culture, *sleep deprivation* is a major issue. Some studies label this situation as epidemic.

If you have PTSD it is even more of a problem because of your increased adrenalin level. And caffeine and sugar only compound the issue. That goes back to diet, but if you make changes there, then you are already reducing at least your sugar intake. Sadly, coffee is not a food group, so it needs to be controlled, too. But you will be surprised at how easy this is if you just pay attention to how often you refill your cup. Make it a conscious act instead of an automatic one (*intention* once again). Not only will this have a positive affect upon your body, mind, and sleeping habits, but you will appreciate it more.

Aside from this, there are active steps you can take to encourage better rest. Begin by turning the lights down an hour or so before your regular bedtime. This will signal your brain that it is time to wind things down. Review your body and how it feels as if you had a checklist. Do some breathing exercises, and connect relaxing your muscles to this. This will also help you let go of the stress of your day. If I did not do these things, I would never sleep.

Skip the high drama TV; you don't need that kind of stimulation. Make your music choices calm and relaxing, and save the stimulating conversations for dinner. Eat that dinner, which is usually our heaviest meal, as early as possible before bedtime.

The idea is to clear the slate of your daily life so that your evening isn't just one more stressor that sloshes over into the quiet time that is supposed to prepare your brain and body for rest. With this help your subconscious can do its part better.

Of course there can still be problems. You are, after all, trying to reorganize how you live your whole life. But this is another place meditation can be useful. Use it to help quiet the thoughts and activities that fill your head and keep you from sleeping. Or, if your mind is too full and even meditation can't help shut it down, try to empty it into the pages of your journal.

How much sleep we need varies from person to person. I have an eighty-two year old friend who has slept four hours a night for years, and is still in perfect health as he works eight to ten hours a day, five days a week. There is no way I could do that. I need my seven, or I'm exhausted. But you can see the range there. Identify where you fit in that, and apply the techniques that will help you achieve it.

Other Helpful Tools

I use a variety of modalities to help my clients. *Vibrational medicine* is one. Vibrational medicine is based on the premise that we are composed of interconnected fields of energy, like chakras. Its use is to balance and soothe the energy and aura of the body. I find that vibrational medicine works well with my more sensitive clients, the ones who are most easily influenced by the moods and attitudes of others, and whose nervous systems have been severely damaged by the impact of their experiences.

Reiki is another. Reiki means, "spiritually guided life force energy." Practitioners use the palms of their hands to direct energy into clients for healing. I have attained the rank of Reiki Master Teacher, which is the highest degree. I love it for the calm and gentleness it imparts to the recipient. It is obviously similar to the "laying on of hands," and I believe this is something anyone can do, even without formal training. Anytime you touch another with pure intent to help them heal you are accessing healing touch. Intention is everything in this. You can even do it for yourself.

Chakra originates from Hindu and Buddhist concepts. Chakras are energy centers or vortices in our bodies. We have seven major chakras and several minor ones. The minor ones in the palms of our hands are how we transfer or direct energy into another. The seven major ones are as follows.

1)   Root Chakra

This gives you your sense of security in the world, and your connection to the earth. It is located at the base of your tailbone (the coccyx), and it is said to be the color red. It governs your adrenal glands, the lower portion of your body, and bone strength. If you have trauma or abuse issues, the root chakra is likely the most important to calm by creating a sense of security in yourself. Its element is earth. Walking is a good way to calm the root chakra.

2) Sacral Chakra

This center gives you your creativity and sexuality. It is located just below your navel. The color associated with it is orange. It governs all the circulatory systems in the body. Drinking plenty of water and dance are just two ways of working with the sacral chakra.

3) Navel (or Solar Plexus) Chakra

This chakra gives you your sense of self, your drive and ambition, and your sensitivities. Located in the solar plexas, it governs digestions and your autonomic nervous system. It is especially important to the three responses, Fight, Flight, and Freeze. If your abuse or trauma was perpetrated by another human being, this energy center is likely damaged. Improving your self-image in your own eyes, and overcoming helplessness and hopelessness strengthen it.

4) Heart Chakra

The heart chakra gives you love and a sense of humanity. It is located in the center of your chest. It governs your heart, lungs, and immune system. Its color is green. To exercise it, practice giving of yourself to others, whether it is by friendship, assistance, or kindness.

5) Throat Chakra

This one gives you your voice in the world (not just the one that makes noise). It is located in the hollow of your throat, just above the clavicle. Its color is sky blue. It governs both your voice and breathing. Its best exercise is to learn to think before you speak, and then do so honestly and tactfully. Also, writing to express yourself and deep breathing are useful.

6) Third Eye Chakra

Located between the eyebrows, this is the source of your intuition and wisdom. It governs sight and sense of smell. When you think of it, think of the color indigo. Just because you can't see it, don't underestimate it. To work with this center, learn to meditate, sit in silence, and listen to your inner self. Strengthen it by actively learning new things.

7) Crown Chakra

This chakra is located at the top of your head, or just above it, of course. This is your conduit and connection to god and the universe. Imagine it as white or gold light, radiating in all directions. It influences every part of your physical and spiritual being. Meditation and prayer strengthen it, as does the effort put into trying to be the best person you can be.

These are our major energy centers. You can lay one hand on your heart chakra and the other at the solar plexus to calm yourself. Drawing energy through my crown chakra, I focus my breath and the appropriate color through those centers, and any of the others, to clear them. If I sense that a center is weakened or congested, I work on them as above, and also with visualization and affirmations.

No matter what you need to do or how you need to use your energy centers, always start by drawing energy through your crown chakra. Because it is your direct connection to the universe or god, it is hardest to damage, and easiest to heal.

When certain people drain your energy, it is through either your heart or your navel chakra. You can recognize who does this to you because you will be exhausted after every encounter you have with them. If this is unacceptable, one technique to counter this (short of avoidance) is to imagine a cord of energy that connects the two of you. Then cut it.

You can know when your aura has damage by the ease in which you are pulled out of balance by other people and external situations. Protect yourself by surrounding yourself with your bubble (Aura Shield) and chakra breathing. Meditate and cut cords if you need to.

Flower Essences

Edward Bach believed that we have thirty-eight soul vibrations, and that many of our problems originated when we blocked certain of these. He believed that flowers had certain individual powers, and that dew collected from the petals of these flowers retained the vibrations and healing powers of the plant. He taught that ingesting the dew, or simply having it in your energy, would help unblock the affected energy. They are primarily used for emotional and spiritual support, and are considered to be both homeopathic and vibrational in use and nature.

I have used Bach Flower Remedies for years. Their effects are cumulative and subtle. I do not personally dispense them to any of my clients, although I am always willing to discuss their merits and point those interested towards more information. But, because the introduction of remedies into ones aura has beneficial effects, I do sometimes use them as "raindrops," from an eyedropper, upon skin or clothes.

I even treat my pets, when needed. Bach's trademarked Rescue Remedy is especially useful for its calming effects on stress, pet or human. It helps to clear that energy.

Homeopathics

Bach Flower Remedies are related to homeopathics. As I am neither a homeopath nor a naturopath, I do not use them in my practice, but I do for my pets and myself. Homeopathic theory holds that taking in the energy of what ails you in the form of tiny white pills that contain minute decoctions of the illness helps build immunity. The basic principle of homeopathy is called "the law of similars," wherein "like is cured by like."

For instance, an herb, arnica, is the homeopathic remedy used to overcome trauma. It is also available as a topical for sore and bruised muscles. But note that it is not safe to ingest arnica in any form except as a prepared homeopathic remedy. There is only a trace amount of arnica (or any other substance) in these pills, and so is not likely to do harm. And, as a topical, use it only as directed on the package, and do not put on broken skin.

Essential Oils

Aromatherapy can be very powerful. It embraces the theory that certain smells from the oils gathered from assorted plants and flowers have strong mental, emotional, and spiritual healing abilities. I have incorporated essential oils into my practice almost since the beginning. I prefer the blends bottled by Young Living. Release, Peace, and Valor are favorites and staples in my office. They are expensive, but they last a long time. A few drops in a carrier oil like grape seed or jojoba oil goes a long way.

Laying On Of Stones

When I worked in a rock shop to learn silversmithing and stone cutting, I collected a lot of powerful stones and pretty rocks. As they are directly connected with the earth, they channel the earth's great healing powers. Get rocks the color of each chakra and place them in the various chakra centers. Decide for yourself if this helps balance and calm you.

If you would like to explore the concepts of this chapter more fully, there are dozens of amazing books in print on each topic. In matters such as these, self-education is a good way to go.

In all respects to the information I have promoted, and that available from other sources, I would be remiss if I did not point out that clinical trials have found no efficacy in or support for the claims made by practitioners. All I can say is that they work for me. Vibrational medicine is a gentle way to support the changes you wish to make. It is about energy and, in the end, that is all we are.

Religion and Spirituality

I would not have survived in the healthy form I now have had I not, from my very beginning, a very strong sense of God. Sometimes I could feel God around me. Always, I could feel God in me. My spiritual self has been my comfort, my home, and my solace.

I have never been a "religious" woman. Religion, in all its traditional forms, has always been too confining and dogmatic for me. However, I have known some religious women and men who embody my vision of truly holy souls. For them, their religion is their expression of spirituality, and their souls shine for it.

I grew up under the gentle influence of my grandfather's spiritual guidance. I was encouraged to and allowed to know God in my own way. My grandfather was interested in metaphysics and psychic abilities and experiences, and nurtured this in me. For anyone who would idolize or envy these abilities, I can only say that they have caused me more pain than not. I rarely access them, because they can provide too much information, and that can be a greater problem than none at all.

Ultimately, Buddhism has been the restful haven for my soul. Even before I found it in Buddhism, it had been my belief that we are in school while we inhabit Earth and life. We come here to grow and evolve as souls.

In Buddhism we choose our parents, our lives, and other significant elements to help us learn specific things. Or we come to help others. This is to help us in our spiritual quest for perfection.

So I had to ask myself why I would choose to incarnate with such a family and have such experiences. The answer is, of course, to do this with. To help myself grow. To help others do the same.

Your spiritual self can be a wonderful, comfortable place to spend time. So go to what calls your soul and find comfort and healing there. Take these tools with you.

Now, there are readers who are thoroughly sick of my foray into spirituality and religion. They do not believe in, or simply reject as implausible, the notion of god in any form or by any name. This is understandable. When we look around the world, when we know the terrible things that have been done to us, it is difficult to reconcile the idea of a munificent deity with the dark reality we know.

Nevertheless, two separate paths can arrive at the same destination. Your path will be the one whereby you believe in yourself, and be the best you can be.

And for those of us who walk the middle of the road, there is always Albert Camus's advice; "I would rather live my life as if there is a God and die to find out there isn't, than live my life as if there isn't and die to find out there is."

That's a surprise none of us need. Find your moral compass and follow it. That should keep most gods, real or imagined, happy.

Community

We are designed for tribal living. This is how we have lived for most of human history. It is only relatively recently - at most, the last thousand years or so - that we have lost or abandoned those roots, and not necessarily for the better. I encourage you to discover the "tribe" you belong to.

My tribe includes all "my" children (those I teach and treat), some good friends, a cousin, a husband and the family I married in to, a couple of daughters and grandchildren, and the Sisters of Charity of Leavenworth, Kansas.

(The story about my involvement with the sisters is long, and too much a digression for the purpose of this work. In brief, I stumbled upon the Sisters of Charity more than a decade ago, and they have truly been a blessing to me. They instill in me a sense of purpose and grace, and, most importantly, a sense of belonging to a community. My work with them, melding my skills to their causes and charism, has broadened and strengthened my own purpose. I will be forever grateful and indebted to them for this.)

Tribal culture provides a complete circle, with all the generations working together. In its simplest expression, a child is born and the grandparents care for it while the parents work. Everyone has a role to play that serves the greater good of the clan and tribe.

I had the joy of this experience to a degree. I have fond memories of my maternal grandparents babysitting us while our parents worked. This is when I was safest. In normal family circumstances, it is a lovely way to bring generations together. I appreciated the love, wisdom, and patience of my grandparents. Because of them a part of me has always been whole, in spite of the detrimental influence of other situations.

But I think that our current culture encourages us to believe that we don't need other people. In this way some of us have learned not to need. Or, at least, to believe that we do not need others.

The tapestry of my life has been boldly and softly colored by many characters who have given me some part of themselves to carry forward in my own life in my own way. This molds and shapes my present and my future. I choose them with care, or they choose me. Either way, I am better for it.

Now I choose people who are happy and mentally and emotionally healthy. People who consistently demonstrate admirable qualities, and that I feel a kinship with. People with whom I feel safe.

You belong among other members of the human race. You are already an important part of tribes, small and large. Finding your place in them is as essential to your healing process as learning to reprogramming your "pathways." A sense of community offers the same comfort as grandma's overstuffed chair.

There is something to be said about giving back to the world. It pays for itself in deep and rich ways. Be available to someone who needs it, make someone smile, or help improve the quality of a life, whether it's feeding birds, picking up a little trash, or spending time with some forgotten old person. You will be uplifted by it. There is so much work to be done; more than anyone can do alone. But our power comes from our numbers. Join causes that you believe in, and see how much more gets done.

Doing for others is powerful medicine for curing what ails you. It helps you realize that you are not alone. You already belong to something larger than yourself: The world. Find a part of it that you can give yourself to, both for its sake and your own.

Healthy Relationships

As you have seen, I had very little idea what a healthy relationship looked like when I was growing up. But I am lucky in that I got to know healthy people whose examples showed me what I was missing and what I needed to look for. I studied them and developed my own menu of how to be. Some of these people knew how to coax my buried goodness out of me and, as I learned to trust them, I was able to let them. Others were simply good friends. And a few just loved me.

I wasn't very good at picking men. I wasn't healthy in mind or spirit, so mostly I found abusive and controlling men; men much like my father. The final straw was the nut-job I attracted, and then had a hell of a time getting rid of, once I realized what I had done to myself. Again. At this point, I decided that I would rather spend my life alone than in a bad and sick relationship. It took work to come to terms with this. It took more to get comfortable with it. But soon enough I found that I no longer feared being on my own, and that awareness set me free. I spent a year like that. No boyfriends; just friends.

So, of course, I met Mr. Right.

He wasn't that at first. He wasn't looking for a relationship any more than I was. So we were new friends that became best friends. Occasional dinner companions. Someone to go see a movie with, or on a picnic in the mountains. Someone I could call on to give me a lift, because I didn't drive. Someone who was kind and cared and listened.

After about a decade of this, he became my husband. And even after more than two decades, he is still my best friend.

This isn't a fairy tale with Happily-Ever-After guaranteed. Even this relationship takes work and maintenance, and even people without my background forget to do this. But because I learned to work so hard at healing myself, I have the skills and determination that even the healthiest relationships require. You are probably sick of hearing it by now, but relationships, like your healing, take work. You can't let yourself be with just anyone because you are afraid of being alone. You have to protect yourself and your healing process, by rejecting the ones who aren't right for you. Prepare yourself to be alone, perhaps even forever. Oddly enough, this may be just the opening a winner needs.

You should be with someone who is truly a friend.

This is the first and most important thing I have learned about healthy relationships:

In a healthy relationship, the participants don't deliberately hurt each other.

This isn't to say that it does not happen. We all say and do things that hurt our partner's feelings. But healthy, caring people do not do this on purpose. In fact, they put a lot of work (there's that word again) into *not* deliberately hurting each other.

Another thing we do in healthy relationships is to overlook the smaller faults. If there is something little that he or she does that gets on your nerves, you can bet that there is something you do that bugs them. But you can't sweat the small stuff, because there is plenty of big stuff to go around. Save your energy for the larger things that the two of you can work on together.

In my life, we take space from one another when we are angry, then discuss the issue later when we both have had time to reflect on it. We always try to show each other every kindness, and gently speak our concerns. My husband and I are both free-spirited individuals, so we don't tell each other what to do. We talk about what we might be planning, and then ask for or offer suggestions. The choice rests with the one who has to live with it. If it is a joint issue we find a compromise we both can live with.

We do not see eye-to-eye on everything, and so we agree to disagree. We are honest with each other and, most importantly, treat each other with respect. And, knowing each other's buttons after all this time, we never, ever deliberately push them.

Our being together has always been a choice based on love, not a have-to coming from fear and loneliness. But neither of us takes even that for granted. Were the unthinkable to arise, and the needs of one of us came to outweigh the needs for us both, then I believe that we would allow the other to depart with grace, because that is who we have become together.

Letting Go

When you are in the process of change and undergoing transitions, often your relationships are, too. It is the nature of change.

Sometimes there is no saving a relationship. This is especially true if the relationship is one that should not have been started in the first place. If you go into one knowing, for instance, that your partner is a serial abuser, then you shouldn't be surprised when you become the serially abused. There is nothing you can do to change this person.

On the other hand, if you habitually choose partners like this - and you know it - all the power is yours to change yourself. If this means letting go, then you have to find the strength in yourself to do so. That can leave a void, but sometimes in life we are meant to be alone. In my time I learned to love those periods. I filled them with art, friends, poetry, and reflection to get to know myself even better.

Even in the best, most "normal" of lives, it is natural for some relationships to fall by the wayside. It is even more likely when you are in the process of changing the patterns of your life and your way of being. There are always people in our lives, especially if we are damaged, who resent our ambition to heal and make ourselves better than we are. These are the ones that try to stop us. They may also be the ones who have to go. This process is sad and painful, and it leaves an emptiness in us. But better an empty wound than one continually opened and filled with poison. You already know this.

One of my personal rules is to let go of what needs to be let go of. I know it when I see it, and you will learn to if you don't already. It's usually when you have tried everything to make something work, and it just doesn't, no matter what you do. I strive to be kind and honest in these situations, but that hasn't always been possible. If it is not, then I prefer avoidance to confrontation. Once again: The only behavior you are responsible for is your own. You can't change someone who doesn't want, or thinks he needs, to change. It is a waste of your personal and spiritual energy that you need for yourself. Call it self-preservation or selfishness if you need to. Just don't give it away, because the more you give, the more they will take, and you end up back where you started.

Contrariwise, if I am being let go by someone, even if I don't know why, I don't try to hold on. I assume they have made a decision that is best for them. I try to fade from their lives with grace and dignity, to ease my discomfort as well as theirs. I have no desire to be where I am not wanted, and I believe in freedom of choice for everyone.

All these things may be occurring at the same time, and will be stressful. Just keep in mind that, at some point, you will finally land on solid ground. When you do, you will see that you have a good foundation to build on.

A Note - Part 1: To Abusers

I cannot sympathize with your way of being in the world. But, to a small degree, I do understand it.

Sometimes the abused come to identify with the abuser. As a matter of survival they may befriend, and even come to love, their abuser. The longer this lasts, the more the mind is twisted into believing that this is the correct way to be.

Or there is the helpless rage that has built up because of the abuse that they don't know how to deal with. Their only release is to lash out at others with the same violence they experienced.

They become the monster that tormented them.

Maybe this is what happened to you. As I said above, I understand it because it could have happened to me. But I made different choices and stopped the cycle.

This isn't to say that I do not believe that there are bad, evil people in the world, who willfully and knowingly abuse the helpless. These are the ones that no amount of New-Agey self-help can redirect. Tribes banished them from their midst. Now we incarcerate some of them when we catch them.

But to hurt someone as a result of your own pain is a different thing, and it *can* be helped. This book is for you almost as much as it is for your victims. Healing yourself is the first step to mending your sins against others.

A Note - Part 2: To Pedophiles and Rapists

These are not acceptable behaviors, and this is as mildly as I can put it. No one "has it coming." It is not your "right." There is no excuse or justification for this behavior. The society you are a part of has set clear boundaries around both of these behaviors. If you have not gotten that message, then you are either too stupid to breathe without instructions, or you are truly sick. Neither is a Get-Out-Of-Jail-Free card. When you get caught, that's where you go. The tribe banishes you. Either is beyond the scope of this book to fully address.

But just like the issues of victims that I have spoken to, your so-called "preferences" must be addressed by self-regulation. When you fantasize about children, when you daydream about rape, you are only reinforcing dangerous and self-destructive neural pathways. "I can't help it" is not a defense. Your brain is yours to control. When you catch yourself going down the path of wrong-thinking, cut it off. Distract yourself with a pre-selected activity if you must. Better yet, call your therapist. Do whatever it takes to keep from ruining innocent lives, and your own.

Final Notes and Thoughts

I wrote this book for you out of my own sense of humanity. It took me twelve years. My research took me into dark, harsh realms of human behavior that would trigger me and cause me to disassociate. Even the act of writing it has triggered my issues at times. But I always came back to it, though, because of you.

When I found my way out of my history, I knew that I had a story to share that that was bigger than myself. I knew that I could come into your life and world, and that I could help you, give you a roadmap out of your history, so that you did not have to spend the rest of your life "reinventing the wheel" of healing.

Healing takes time. But it doesn't matter how long it takes, as long as you have that as a goal to strive for. Do it in your own time; but do it.

I wish you a wonderful journey back to yourself. I have offered you what I believe to be effective tools, tested in the laboratory of myself. Use them as a starting place to find even more that work for you, wherever your spirit feels moved to search; books, healers, or in your sense of god.

Peace be with you. And, at last, peace can be with me.

Recommended Reading

Following is a list of titles that I often suggest to my clients. Some are the product of complex and scholarly research by masters in particular disciplines. Others are more readable.

The Power of Focusing: A Practical Guide to Emotional Self-Healing. Ann Weiser Cornell, Ph.D.

The Body Bears the Burden: trauma, Disassociation, and Disease. Robert C. Scaer.

Quantum Healing: Exploring the Frontiers of Body/Mind Medicine. Deepak Chopra.

A Handbook of Chakra Healing: Spiritual Practice for Health, Harmony and Inner Peace. Kalashatra Govinda.

Essential Reiki: A Complete Guide to an Ancient Healing Art. Diane Stein.

Adrenal Fatigue: the 21st Century Stress Syndrome. James L. Wilson, N.D., D.C., Ph.D.

Post-trauma Stress: Reduce Long-term Effects and Hidden Emotional Damage Caused by Violence and Disaster. Frank Parkinson.

The Cortisol Connection: Why Stress Makes You Fat and Ruins Your Health - and What You can Do About It. Shawn M. Talbot, Ph.D.

The Hidden Link Between Adrenaline and Stress: The Exciting New Breakthrough that Helps You Overcome Stress Damage. Dr. Archibald D. Hart.

The Body Remembers: The Psychophysiology of Trauma and Trauma Treatment. Babette Rothschild.

Trauma and Recovery: The Aftermath of Violence - from Domestic Abuse to Political Terror. Judith Herman, M.D.

Touching: The Human Significance of Skin. Ashley Montegu.

Healing the Child Within: Discovery and Recovery for Adult Children of Dysfunctional Families. Charles L. Witfield, M.D.

The Breaking of Bodies and Minds: Torture, Psychiatric Abuse, and the Health Professions. Eric Stover.

Why Zebras Don't Get Ulcers: Un Updated Guide to Stress, Stress related Diseases, and Coping (2nd Edition). Robert M. Sapolsky.

Boundaries - Where You End and I Begin: How to Recognize and Set Healthy Boundaries. Anne Katherine, M.A.

After the Darkest Hour: How Suffering Begins the Journey to Wisdom. Kathleen A. Brehony, Ph.D.

Body, Self, and Soul: Sustaining Integration. Jack Lee Rosenberg, D.D.S., Ph.D; Majories L. Rand, Ph.D; and Diane Asay, M.A.

Energy Vampires: A Practical Guide for Psychic Self-Protection. Dorothy Harbor.

Touch Starvation in America: A Call to Arms. Denny Johnson.

The Bach Flower Remedies. Edward Bach and E.J. Wheeler.

The Courage to Heal: A Guide for Women Survivors of Child Sexual Abuse. Ellen Bass and Laura Davis.